ENDORSEMENTS From Teachers

"This book is easy to read and easy to relate it. It provides small, tangible steps that can be implemented by any teacher or parent. It is the 'scaffold' that educators have been looking for to set the stage for tremendous learning."

—**Brenda Harari,** Ph.D., Educational Researcher and Consultant

"This book shows teachers how to strengthen relationships, fuel interest, passion, and inspire accomplishment! The authors solve the age-old mystery of how to resolve classroom conflicts without disrupting the learning process."

—**Resa Brown,** Special Education Teacher of the Year

"*The Compassionate Classroom* presents clear and concise explanations of the 'how' and 'why' of Nonviolent Communication along with playful exercises and games that animate the joy of natural giving. I am confident that *The Compassionate Classroom* will inspire many students in my college classes to share NVC in their own classrooms and beyond."

—**Michael Dreiling,** Sociology Professor and Author

"*The Compassionate Classroom* has great exercises and practical lessons that give educators tools to implement Nonviolent Communication in the classroom and create connections with students that will enhance both learning and teaching."

—**Leslie Trook,** Middle School Principal

"I am excited by *The Compassionate Classroom* and its potential to help the conflict that is a daily reality in our schools, especially here in South Africa. Some of its exercises and games have already yielded interesting results in our classes. It is an invaluable practical tool for today's teacher. I heartily recommend it."

—**Shena Lamb,** University Instructor

"*The Compassionate Classroom* is a highly accessible, reader-friendly book that delivers what it promises. My dog-eared copy is an invaluable aid in supporting courses I develop and teach, as well as an encouraging, uplifting work. There are two sections; the first describes with certain clarity the power of learning in a 'safe' classroom where children can participate without fear of shame or blame. The second provides practical tools and exercises that are easily duplicated in the classroom. I predict this book will become an indispensable guide for professional educators and parents who strive to create schools where 'learning flourishes and teachers enjoy teaching.' It's a gem!"

—**Marcy Piekos,** Educator

"Last year was the best year of my teaching career. The tools in this book helped me transform my classroom from an ordinary to an extraordinary learning environment. Some end-of-the-year evaluations from my students said: This has been a really awesome experience! This is such a fun class! Mrs. Adivi is nice and fair. This class is a real treat! You will definitely love this class! One year ago I wouldn't have thought these kinds of statements were possible."

—**Carla Adivi,** 7th Grade Science Teacher

"Visionary and practical, insightful and inviting, *The Compassionate Classroom* will touch the heart and enhance the practice of all who read it."

—**Rob Koegel**, Associate Professor of Sociology

"The language of Nonviolent Communication is a very clear and usable tool and replaces the language of shame, guilt, and blame. The authors demonstrate how this language introduces cooperation and peace into the classroom, and consequently, into the world. Supported by scientific research that shows how emotional clarity and ease enhance children's ability to learn, the authors give various examples of how to learn and teach this process, adding a number of fun classroom exercises and games.

This book is not just for teachers—anyone interested in compassionate interactions will benefit."

—**Marcelline Brogli,** Therapist and Teacher Consultant

The Compassionate Classroom

Relationship Based Teaching and Learning

Sura Hart and Victoria Kindle Hodson

2240 Encinitas Blvd., Ste. D-911, Encinitas, CA 92024

email@PuddleDancer.com • www.PuddleDancer.com

The Compassionate Classroom:
Relationship Based Teaching and Learning

A PuddleDancer Press Book

PuddleDancer Press, Permissions Dept.
2240 Encinitas Blvd., Ste. D-911, Encinitas, CA 92024
Tel: 760-652-5754 Fax: 760-274-6400
www.NonviolentCommunication.com Email@PuddleDancer.com

Ordering Information
Please contact Independent Publishers Group,
Tel: 312-337-0747; Fax: 312-337-5985;
Email: frontdesk@ipgbook.com or visit
www.IPGbook.com for other contact information
and details about ordering online

Authors: Sura Hart and Victoria Kindle Hodson
Cover Design: Lightbourne, Inc.
Interior Design: MGM Graphic Design

Manufactured in the United States of America

1st Printing, October 2004

10 9 8 7 6 5

Paperback ISBN: 978-1-892005-06-9
eBook ISBNs: 978-1-934336-02-1 (ePUB), 978-1-892005-78-6 (mobi) 978-1-892005-45-8 (PDF)

Compassion is not a static state, nor is it a destination to be reached. Compassion is not a subject that can be taught. Compassion is a way of being in relationship—a way of acting and interacting. At the same time, certain practices can help cultivate this way of being. In our experience, Nonviolent Communication is the most practical and powerful of these practices.

—Sura Hart and Victoria Kindle Hodson

Contents

Acknowledgments

We would like to acknowledge, with deep appreciation, the following contributors to this book:

Our students and fellow teachers who, by daily gifts of honesty, trust, and kindness, gave roots to our understanding and appreciation of the power of relationship based teaching and learning;

Marshall Rosenberg, for creating and sharing the process of Nonviolent Communication that is at the heart of *The Compassionate Classroom* and for inspiring us to contribute to the growing body of NVC work;

Gary Baran, Executive Director, and the Board of Directors of the Center for Nonviolent Communication, for vision, passion, and support;

The New Earth Foundation, the Threshold Foundation, and many individual donors who believed in this project and provided essential financial support for it;

Our editors and consultants, Gary Baran, John Dobrzanski, Kyra Freestar, Rita Herzog, Stanley Hodson, and Rob Koegel, who spent many hours reading through various drafts of the manuscript and offered wonderful suggestions for improvement along with unwavering encouragement and support;

Marty and Lisa Mellein, who contributed artistic vision, talent, and a great deal of flexibility working with us;

The CNVC Education Project Steering Committee, John Cunningham, Jillian Froebe, Sylvia Haskvitz, Liv Monroe, and Jean Morrison, for their vision, passion, numerous rounds of empathy throughout the writing of this book, and their many labors of love;

The CNVC Education Project Team members who first conceived of a book for teachers and then contributed activities, ideas, and inspiration: Martine Algier, Diane Arrigoni, Katie Barak, Marcelline Brogli, Doug Dolstad, Marilyn Fiedler, Marianne Gothlin, Holley Humphrey, Mary Mackenzie, Marlene Marskornick, Natasha Rice, Allan Rohlf, Robin Rose, Jean Ryan, and Fred Sly.

Meiji Stewart, Neill Gibson, and Shannon Bodie—the PuddleDancer Press team—who have taken us step by step through this book, generously sharing their skill, knowledge, and good humor.

Letter From the Authors to Teachers

Dear Teachers,

Do you want to know why your students resist your best teaching efforts, bully one another, and don't want to do their school work?

The Compassionate Classroom: Relationship Based Teaching and Learning uncovers the truth behind these behaviors and gives you tools and skills to make learning and compassion thrive in your classroom.

We suggest you use this book as a tutorial to:

- take a closer look at the four kinds of relationships in your classroom
- determine whether your classroom is a safe place
- learn how to motivate students without punishment or reward
- recognize defiance, bullying, and underachievement as symptoms of a deeper cause
- practice a way to communicate that eliminates fear and fosters trust
- unlock your students' natural desire to learn

Use the exercises and activities to help your students:

- learn how to resolve conflicts
- cooperate to meet mutual needs
- take responsibility for their learning

We hope ***The Compassionate Classroom*** contributes new depth to your teaching and learning.

With best wishes,
Sura and Victoria

Introduction

Writing *The Compassionate Classroom: Relationship Based Teaching and Learning* has been a collaborative process that has enriched our lives in many ways. We have brought our collective forty-five years of teaching experience to the task of sharing how compassion and learning can blossom in the classroom. We have unpacked the foundational premises of Nonviolent Communication℠ (NVC℠) and framed the process in terms that teachers can readily share with young people. In making this book available, we hope to introduce teachers and parents to a process that powerfully integrates the intelligence of the mind with the intelligence of the heart. Our greatest desire is to provide teachers with practical tools to help them bring more lively learning and compassion into their classrooms.

Nonviolent Communication is both a consciousness of our compassionate nature and a process for interacting. As we wrote about NVC, we tried to clearly express the nature of this process and the nuances of the language without being formulaic or implying that there's a right way to communicate. As a result, our understanding of NVC has deepened greatly. The challenge of describing an open-ended, creative, improvisational process of interacting still stretches our imaginations and capabilities. We are deeply grateful to Marshall Rosenberg for developing Nonviolent Communication and stretching the hearts of people all around the world toward a more enlivened, compassionate way of living.

Marshall Rosenberg developed Nonviolent Communication because he wanted to see more compassion in human relations. In his early training and practice in clinical psychology, he became acutely aware of the negative effects of diagnostic labeling and realized the power of language to shape thinking and consciousness. He studied the major spiritual traditions, paying attention to the language used by people whose lives emanated the love and compassion at the heart of these teachings. From his study

Dr. Rosenberg concluded that creating a peaceful world entails eliminating language that blames, shames, criticizes, and demands—language based on habitual thinking that inhibits compassion and contributes to violence. He developed a way of using language that connects us to the heart of human experience—values, dreams, desires, and needs. This clarity helps people meet their own needs and joyfully contribute to meeting the needs of others.

Marshall Rosenberg first used NVC in federally funded projects in the United States to provide mediation and communication skills training for racial integration in schools. Since then he has spread this powerful peace-making process worldwide. He has offered mediation and training in war-torn countries including Israel, the Palestinian Authority, Rwanda, Sri Lanka, Croatia, Serbia, Colombia, Sierra Leone, and Burundi. In 1985 he started the Center for Nonviolent Communication (CNVC), an international organization with trainers throughout the world who teach in schools, prisons, health care facilities, and government agencies.

In 1999, CNVC launched an Education Project to develop materials for schools and trainings for educators. This project has been generously supported by grants from the New Earth Foundation and the Threshold Foundation, as well as by donations from many individuals. *The Compassionate Classroom* is an outcome of the CNVC Education Project.

◆

We wrote this book for educators, particularly for elementary school teachers. We hope that the insights, tools, activities, and resources in it will support teachers who are, or would like to be, nurturing the seeds of compassion in their classrooms. We have been listening to teachers for many years. While writing this book, however, we found ourselves listening more closely than ever to their dreams, their concerns, and their frustrations. Their voices have guided us from cover to cover, and we begin this book with *Appreciation: Listening to Teachers.*

Section I explains how relationships impact teaching and learning and focuses on four vital relationships in the classroom: teacher to self, teacher to student, student to student, and student to learning. When we tend these relationships and infuse them with mutual respect, we nurture seeds of compassion.

Section II offers practical tools for creating a Compassionate Classroom. Five premises help develop a consciousness of our compassionate nature, which is at the heart of Nonviolent Communication. The distinct components of the NVC process offer guidelines for learning a language of compassion. Four dialogues convey the power of this language in classroom interactions. A variety of activities and games created by teachers provide skill development and practice. A Guide to Lesson Planning gives suggestions for how to quickly combine exercises and activities in this book to create lesson plans.

We hope that readers of *The Compassionate Classroom* are inspired to learn and practice Nonviolent Communication and to discover for themselves how their lives and relationships are enriched.

Appreciation: Listening to Teachers

We talked with many teachers during the writing of this book. Their concerns and delights often echoed one another. They were excited when they spoke of their desire to nourish student growth. They expressed frustration, sadness, and a sense of helplessness when they discussed the punitive policies, rules, threats, and rewards that prevail in their schools. They often stressed how discouraged they feel when students' needs are not addressed. In the next few pages you will hear the teachers speak for themselves.

With reference to rules, consequences, and punishment, one teacher who works in a large elementary school in Washington State lamented:

> It's so painful for me to witness the system that is in place [rules, consequences, and punishments]. Children are not encouraged to explore what needs they are trying to meet by behaving the ways they do. They don't get to explore other alternatives to their behavior, the impact that their behavior had on others, or ways to make amends. I do what I can, but the system seems so big, and there is so much history to those punitive practices that I feel despair when I think about trying to change them. It's painful to see young children, every day, subjected to those practices.

A woman who teaches conflict resolution several hours a week in an elementary school said:

> I am so discouraged, not just about the system but about myself. I have great compassion for the kids, but I have so many judgments about the teachers and parents. I see what they do. I hear what they say. And, I just want to scream, "Damn it, can't you see what you're doing?" We have these things called "consequences" that are really punishments. Many, many times faculty and parents say to me: "You're so wonderful. The work you do is so important." But it's as if they are really saying, "You're going to fix our kids for us, aren't you?" I'm not going to punish their kids, and I want them to understand how ineffective consequences and punishments are. I have no idea how to proceed.

Talking about teacher creativity and innovation, another teacher felt excited about experimenting with what he saw as "life serving systems" in his classroom:

> I never used force. I focused on having students contribute from their own self-described ways of learning. The sad part of it was that I formulated [all my ideas] into a program, and there was no interest from administration in educational innovation, as such. Even though students wrote many testimonials about my contribution, my boss brushed my proposal aside.

A writing teacher expressed her sadness about the emphasis on testing in her school district:

> Everything is based on a test, and I feel so frustrated about that because it doesn't allow the child to shine through. I work around the system that is set in place, and I feel guilty about that. I'm the person who makes a decision that affects the rest of their lives. It all comes down to what number I write on a piece of paper, and that's really frustrating to me.

This teacher's guilt has to do with the fact that she "works around the system" by occasionally raising test scores in order to create important opportunities for students—opportunities that would otherwise be denied to them if their scores were not high enough.

Another teacher put his concerns about testing this way:

> I feel a lot of frustration and anger with the system of assessment required by the state, the federal government's "No Child Left Behind" program, and the principal of my school. They only want to see the norm tests. They don't want to see portfolio assessments, criterion assessments, or other assessments that show **growth** of children. "So what?" they say, "That's frivolous. What did students get on the Stanford 9? What was his grade point average? What was her percentile ranking?" This is what they look at. They take that child and throw that child away and

> look at the numbers. Children know this is happening, and it frustrates me! My empathy is for the children and their needs.

One teacher who works with 500–600 students a week said:

> I think that it's an abuse of human beings for one teacher to teach so many students. I took this year off because I couldn't bear the workload. I want to scream out: "There needs to be a balance. Yes, a teacher is a warrior, but also has a tender, precious life and needs balance and to be able to make a living." I don't think that people realize the silent kind of violence that is going on in our classrooms.

Another teacher with an extremely large student load said:

> I love being able to teach my passion, which is art. I do a lot of self-evaluation with my students. I don't give out rewards. I give a lot of choices. Despite my efforts, I find myself pulled more and more into the domination system. I feel like I'm out there on my own in this monstrous system. I see these kids who absolutely hate school. It's an enormous battle. It's wearing me down.

It is clear that structural changes beyond the scope of the classroom are needed. The focus of this book, however, is on what teachers can do in classrooms, not how the present system came to be or how we could change it. Still, we want to draw attention briefly to what we see as important systemic issues.

In our present school system politicians and administrators make many important decisions and policies that affect what goes on inside classrooms. These top-down decisions are then presented to teachers as rules, policies, and expectations that must be followed and demands that must be met. We see this as a critical flaw of the system: so much of what teachers teach and students learn is forced upon them. Whenever people are forced to do anything, they usually see only two poor choices: to submit and become compliant, apathetic and/or resentful, or to rebel. Coercion in any form undermines the emotional safety necessary for students to learn and for teachers to teach.

We would like to see parents, administrators, teachers, and students have a voice in decision making and address some basic questions: What is the purpose of our present school system? Who decides this? Do we agree with this purpose? What are the policies that are in place? Do these policies meet the needs of students and teachers? If not, what policies would meet these needs more effectively? When these issues are addressed by the entire school community, we *will* find ways to change the system.

Clearly, one teacher cannot change the system by herself. At the same time, we hope to show in this book that by tending *relationships* in classrooms, teachers inevitably become powerful agents of change within the system. People who are clear about their needs are not likely to sit by—apathetic, listless, resentful—while others make decisions for them. They are more likely to take up Gandhi's challenge to "Be the change you want to see in the world."

There is another effect of tending relationships in the classroom: the inevitable increase in respect, cooperation, and learning that results from this tending can be readily felt and seen by those around us. Other teachers and parents begin to wonder and ask what we are doing to create such vitality in our classroom. In this organic way, our circle of influence grows.

As we write, politicians are pushing for more and more standardized testing. At the same time, every day we hear more teachers, administrators, counselors, parents, and students expressing their distress about these practices. We urge people to speak up, to lend their voices to the growing world-wide movement to create life-serving practices in schools that promote autonomy and interdependence, inspire compassionate interactions, and keep alive young people's natural joy of learning. With such practices in place, we believe that our young people will grow into adults who create organizations and governments that will care for and sustain all forms of life on the planet.

Section I

The Relationship-Teaching-Learning Connection

Introduction to Section I

Section I raises two questions: What do teachers and students need in order to thrive—to engage in joyful learning and compassionate interactions? And how can we contribute to meeting these needs? To meet more needs of both teachers and students, we invite educators to bring relationship to the center of classroom concerns. We draw upon contemporary research to support our central assertion that engaged learning only occurs when the needs of teachers and students for physical and emotional safety are met. Establishing safety first engenders the trust that is necessary for each learner to take risks and to be vulnerable enough to participate in the learning process.

This section also introduces four vital relationships in classroom life: a teacher's relationship to herself, a teacher's relationships with her students, students' relationships with one another, and students' relationships with their learning processes and the curriculum. We highlight ways to nurture these relationships that increase safety, learning, and compassion in the classroom.

Chapter 1
Creating Safety and Trust

> Kids learn in communion. They listen to people who matter to them and to whom they matter.
>
> *Nel Noddings*

What *do* teachers and students need and want? Students we talked to often told us that teachers don't listen to them and that all that teachers want is for students to be quiet and to turn in their homework on time. In short, what students say they want most is for teachers and other adults to listen to them, respect their ideas, and consider their needs.

Teachers want students to take more responsibility for their behavior and learning. They want to have more time to give attention to individual learning needs and to see more engaged learning taking place in their classrooms. They want school policies that are more respectful of students and that would encourage more respectful interactions between students. For themselves, they would like to have more respectful interactions with administrators and other policy makers.

To meet the needs of both students and teachers we suggest placing relationships at the center of classroom concern. In a "relationship based" classroom, safety, trust, student needs, teacher needs, and modes of communication are considerations as important as history, language arts, science, or other academic subjects. Teachers may think that these new considerations require more work for them. However, we hope to show that time spent creating safety and trust, meeting individual needs, and improving communication skills actually creates what educators want most—a compassionate learning community where engaged learning flourishes.

The Case for Safety First

Alfie Kohn points out in his book *No Contest* that if we want learning to take place, students need the emotional safety provided by "an environment built upon support, nurturing, consideration, mutual contribution, a sense of belonging, protection, acceptance, encouragement, and understanding"[1]—in other words, a relationship based classroom where needs of students and teachers are respected. In such a classroom there is safety and trust. And where there is safety and trust, there are the seeds for compassion and engaged learning.

> Fear in whatever form prevents the understanding of ourselves and of our relationship to all things.
>
> *J. Krishnamurti*

When teachers consciously create caring relationships and teach relationship skills, they build a strong foundation of safety and trust. Studies show that this increased safety and trust result in more cooperation, less conflict, and fewer verbal put downs in the classroom. Students are more sensitive to the needs of others, and empathy increases between teachers and students as well as between students. In addition, better scores on standardized achievement tests and improved ability to acquire skills have been reported. [2]

Results of a year long study of the effects of teaching NVC to elementary school age children showed improved relationships between students and teacher, reduction of conflicts, increased confidence in communication skills, and, in general, more harmony and cooperation in the school community.[3]

In spite of the evidence showing the importance of safe, trusting relationships, we know that many students and teachers do not feel safe at school. From pressure and stress in classrooms to playground conflicts, there is much about school life that contributes to anxiety and fear. Physical violence on school campuses is the most obvious sign that there is a lack of safety for students. The fear that these incidents engender has profound effects for students and their families.

Many parents we have spoken to are afraid to send their children to schools and are choosing to homeschool them. A guidance counselor in a Southern California junior high school told us that, for the first time in her twenty-five-year career, she is working with students who are so fearful about their physical safety at school that they refuse to attend. This phenomenon is taking place in schools throughout the United States. The National Education Association reports that 160,000 students stay home from school every day due to fear of attack or intimidation.

While acts of physical violence cause general alarm and concern for the safety of our children, there are less dramatic daily occurrences at school that induce fear in students by undermining their *emotional* safety. As a result of the compulsory nature of one-size-fits-all curricula, methods, and school policies, many fourth, fifth, and sixth grade students realize that school is not a place where they will be able to get their needs for understanding, contributing, and learning met. Out of their sense of hopelessness and frustration, some lash out with name calling, verbal put downs, taunting, or other aggressive behaviors. These are counter-productive strategies for meeting fundamental needs. However, bullying in one form or another is a common occurrence in most schools. The Centers for Disease Control and Prevention report that approximately 75 percent of students say they have been bullied at school.

Bullying creates a climate of fear and dread that threatens the physical and emotional safety of all students. It is very difficult to stay focused on studies when you are trying to recover from the altercation you just had or when you are anticipating the next one.

As James Garbarino and Ellen deLara have shown, "Many schools inadvertently support and enable hostile and emotionally violent environments."[4] Although teachers feel discouraged by the daily round of bullying, put downs, taunting, teasing, blaming and cliquish behavior, and recognize the cost to themselves and students, they don't know what to do about it. And all too often they don't even know that they are contributing to it.

Marshall Rosenberg tells the story of a school principal he visited who was looking out at the school playground from his office window. The principal saw a big boy hit a smaller boy. He ran from his office, swatted the bigger boy, and gave him a lecture. When he got back to his office, the principal said, "I taught that fellow not to hit people who are smaller than he is." Dr. Rosenberg said: "I'm not so sure that's what you did. I think that you taught him not to do it while you're looking." The principal did not see that he was modeling the very behavior that he was trying to stop.

Other ways that teachers, often unknowingly, stimulate fear in students include: using labels and comparisons, criticizing, making demands, and threatening punishment. These have become part of the daily climate of school life and are therefore taken for granted. Unrecognized and unchallenged, they provide powerful modeling of behaviors that students will mimic in their interactions. These practices stimulate fear and contribute to excessive stress, under-performance, a wide range of violent behaviors, and high dropout rates in later years.[5]

Our first question should be, "What do children need?". . . followed immediately by "How can we meet those needs?"

From this point of departure we will end up in a very different place than if we had begun by asking, "How do I get children to do what I want?"

Alfie Kohn

Whether students act aggressively toward one another or teachers habitually use aggressive practices to control students, the effects are the same. Fear inducing behaviors of all kinds erode safety and trust, and thus inhibit learning.

The Safety–Learning Connection

Emotional safety and the ability to learn have been correlated in contemporary educational and brain research. This research has shown that the emotional center of the brain is so powerful that negative emotions such as hostility, anger, fear, and anxiety automatically "downshift" the brain to basic, survival thinking. This can make learning very difficult, if not impossible. Under such stress, the neo-cortex or reasoning center of the brain shuts down. In his book *Emotional Intelligence*, Daniel Goleman calls this an "emotional hijacking." Goleman shows that in the presence of strong negative emotions stress hormones are secreted in preparation for fight or flight. The fight or flight response has been understood for a long time, but insight into the effect it has on a student's ability to concentrate, to memorize, and to recall information is relatively new.[6]

Since many students don't experience emotional safety at home, they come to school already stressed and in a "downshifted" state. If they have hostile, discouraging, or otherwise negative interactions with teachers, some students remain in an almost constant state of fight or flight. The brain is so thoroughly preoccupied with survival needs that these students are literally unavailable for the complex activities of the mind that learning requires. Tragically, their curiosity, wonder, and awe have been usurped by a state of heightened vigilance and an immediate need for protection and security.

In addition, as Joseph Chilton Pearce points out, the emotional state that we are in at the moment learning takes place is imprinted as part of that learning and negatively influences recall at a later time.[7] Perhaps you have noticed that some children feel afraid when they are learning the multiplication tables or when they are asked to write something. This fear can block the memory of learning that occurred the day before. Some students we have met suffered such fear and discouragement about writing in early grades of school that they refuse to write for months or sometimes years. Many adults we know still have intense emotions that arise when they are asked to write, to do math problems, or to read aloud.

Doc Lew Childre says, "Fear is beneficial if we are in real danger and need to react fast; but fear limits perception, communication, and learning if we are not in danger."[8] The remainder of this book explores alternatives to fear inducing practices such as: punishment, reward, threats, bribes, moralistic judgments, and comparisons, that are the norm in many schools and families. This book introduces and emphasizes *relationship based* practices and structures that help students and teachers learn "relational power"[9] or *power with* others.

Two Primary Ways to Create Safety and Trust in the Classroom

1. Focus on the Needs of Students and Teachers

Relationships in a classroom are essentially the interplay of needs—needs of the students and needs of the teacher. What needs do students have? What needs do teachers have? According to William Glasser the basic human needs are for survival, power, belonging, freedom, and fun.[10] According to Abraham Maslow they are survival, protection/safety, belonging, competence/learning, and autonomy or self-actualization.[11]

Nonviolent Communication greatly expands the vocabulary of needs. The subject of needs and NVC's unique way of accessing them through feelings are developed at length in Chapters 3 and 4. No matter how we categorize needs, learning is not the *only* need that students bring to school. They bring their needs for belonging, fun, freedom, competence, and autonomy as well. A teacher in a relationship based classroom knows this and treats all of these needs as important. Indeed, unless these needs are acknowledged and met to their satisfaction, students will not feel safe enough to fully engage in the learning process.

William Glasser asks the provocative question, "What if we change the focus [in schools] from disciplining students to meeting needs?" He goes on to say that "students who seem to be very different from each other in academic standing are suddenly the same, since they all have the same needs."[12] The trust level rises markedly when students realize that a relationship based classroom teacher is supporting their common needs rather than ranking their academic differences.

In general, only a child who feels safe dares to grow forward healthily. His safety needs must be gratified. He can't be pushed ahead, because the ungratified safety needs will remain forever underground, always calling for satisfaction.

Abraham Maslow

2. Learn and Practice a Language of Giving and Receiving

Virginia Satir once said, "I see communication as a huge umbrella that covers and affects all that goes on between human beings."[13] If this is true, why is there so little attention to the umbrella? How we communicate our needs and listen to the needs of others determines whether needs are likely to get met. In a relationship based classroom, teachers and students try to become aware of habitual ways of expressing needs and practice new ways of expressing them that are most likely to be heard. They also practice the art of empathy—of listening for their own feelings and needs and those of others. For these purposes, a relationship based classroom uses guidelines for how to communicate with one another. In order for all voices to be heard, no matter how loud or soft, and for there to be sharing without blame or criticism, teachers and students take the time to learn and practice a non-confrontive way of using language.

Members of a relationship based classroom practice skills in "relational intelligence": guessing feelings of others from verbal and non-verbal cues; identifying values—one's own and those of others; translating judgments into statements of feelings and needs or strategies for meeting needs; and taking responsibility for one's own thoughts, feelings, and actions.

Without doubt, a classroom environment of emotional safety and trust is the foundation for learning to take place. To create such an environment it is vitally important to put the study of relationships at the center of the curriculum with the "core" subjects.

We move on now to show you how to turn your classroom into a "relationship based" learning community by revitalizing your thinking and your interactions with yourself, your students, and your curriculum.

Chapter 2
Relationships in the Classroom

> The curious paradox is that when I accept myself just as I am, then I can change.
>
> *Carl Rogers*

There are at least four types of relationships in the classroom: 1) teacher to self, 2) teacher to student, 3) student to student, and 4) student to his or her own learning process. When we notice the dynamics of these relationships and become aware of how our values and actions affect them, we increase the possibilities for creating a compassionate classroom, one interaction at a time.

A word of advice as you read this chapter: Focusing on the dynamics in classroom relationships is likely to stir up many feelings. You might feel sad, disappointed, or discouraged when you see the gap between your actions and what you want for yourself and for your students. However, taking time to notice the discrepancy, *without judging yourself or others*, can bring insight and lead to more effective strategies for creating what you want.

Along the way, we predict that you will also notice that many relationships in your classroom *do support* learning and compassion. We encourage you to take time to celebrate this when you see it. Acknowledging and celebrating successes is one of the powerful, life-serving practices we recommend to all learners.

1. Teacher-Self Relationship

In the important relationship with yourself, we invite you to take time to notice the following:

What is your intention in teaching?

What qualities do you most value in yourself? In others?

What qualities do you want to cultivate in your students?

What kinds of relationships do you want?

What are your interests?

What are your talents?

What are your most effective ways to learn?

True compassion requires us to attend to our own humanity, to come to a deep acceptance of our own life as it is. It requires us to come into right relationship with that which is most human in ourselves.

Rachel Naomi Remen

How Do You Think About Yourself?

A tendency to criticize and judge yourself usually results in being critical of others. Compassion for oneself is more likely to result in compassion for others.

How Do You Think About Your Work and Your Contribution?

Take time to recognize your contributions and track your successes. Take time to look at mistakes so you can learn from them: notice what needs you were trying to meet and consider how you might meet them more effectively next time.

What Do You Really Enjoy Doing and How Often Do You Do It?

Activities that bring genuine joy are rejuvenating. If you aren't having fun in your life, it might be hard to support your students' important need for fun in their lives.

Do You Ask For and Receive Support From Others?

As an educator you give a great deal of yourself to your teaching and to your students. Do you remember to ask for support from others who can listen to you and give you empathy for the countless daily challenges and frustrations that you face? Do you also take the time to celebrate your joys and successes with others?

2. Teacher-Student Relationships

> What we are teaches the child far more than what we say, so we must be what we want our children to become.
>
> *Joseph Chilton Pearce*

If we want our students to think for themselves, to be honest and authentic, we need to be reflective, honest, and authentic ourselves. If we want our students to know that their thoughts and feelings matter to us, we will take the time to listen to them and to consider their points of view. What kind of learners do you want your students to be? Is there a gap between your vision and your practice?

By becoming more aware of how we interact with students, we can see whether or not we are creating relationships that provide safety, generate trust, and encourage learning. At every point of contact we convey how we see students and what we believe they can achieve. What are you conveying to your students? How are you conveying this amid the pressures for students to perform well on standardized tests?

What Is Your Intention?

Do you want to connect with the students or do you want to get things done your way? Parker Palmer, author of *The Courage to Teach*, says that when he has asked students from all around the country to describe a good teacher, all of them described:

> People who have some sort of connective capacity, who connect themselves to their students, their students to each other, and everyone to the subject being studied. . . . The connections made by good teachers are held not in their methods but in their hearts . . . the place where intellect and emotion and spirit and will converge.[1]

Marshall Rosenberg has a way of checking intention by asking, "Are you playing kindness or are you playing who's right?"

How Do You See Your Students?

When your students come through the door, do you see them as whole human beings with their own thoughts, feelings, needs, talents, interests, and gifts to share? If this is so, you are likely to experience feelings of excitement, awe, and curiosity. If, instead, you feel anxious or afraid, you probably have a different image in your mind—maybe one of students as lazy, disruptive, wild, demanding, and/or rebellious. How you think about your students at the beginning and throughout the year often communicates louder than your words.

> Teaching is some kind of connection between people, not rules on a piece of paper.
>
> *John Taylor Gatto*

Nonviolent Communication provides a way to translate all labels into observable behavior and then to understand the needs underlying the behavior. For example, instead of calling a student "lazy," we could simply make the observation that he is nodding off in class and not doing the assigned work. If asked, he might tell us that he is tired and needs more sleep at night. With more conversation we might discover that he has a new baby sister who wakes him up with her crying.

Do You See Each Child's Gifts?

More than anything else, we each want to contribute to life—to share our gifts. Our gifts vary widely; everyone has unique contributions to make. Your keenness for recognizing students' gifts and receiving them allows every student to contribute, which may be the greatest gift that you can give them. There is a Swahili proverb that says, "The greatest gift we can give others is not just to share our riches with them, but to reveal their riches to themselves."

What Is Your Body Language?

Speaking and listening eye-to-eye with students is a suggestion that is easy to implement, but only if we remember to do it. Regardless of how short a child is, we can squat or sit down to talk with him in this respectful way. We can invite students who are taller than we are to sit down so that we can talk eye-to-eye with them, too.

How Often Do You Listen? How Often Do You Speak?

Listening carefully to students shows that we value what they say and take them seriously. It contributes to understanding, connection, and trust. If teachers could make only one change in a classroom, making a shift to listening more is probably the most important. Again and again, students say this is what they want most.

What Are You Listening For?

Are you listening for the needs that your students have? Are you listening for the feelings that students have? Do you encourage students to grow themselves from the inside out by formulating and asking lots of questions, drawing their own conclusions, and constructing their own theories? Do you take their questions seriously and trust that they can find their own answers? Or, is the classroom primarily a platform for the textbooks' answers and for your knowledge and opinions?

Power is of two kinds. One is obtained by fear of punishment, and the other by acts of love. Power based on love is a thousand times more effective and permanent than the one derived from fear of punishment.

Gandhi

What Do You Do When a Student Says "No"?

In their attempts to meet their needs, your students are always saying "Yes" to something. It's easy to enjoy their "Yes" when it's in response to something you want them to do. It's more difficult and very important to hear what they're saying "Yes" to when they're doing something you don't want them to do, or when they say "No" to your requests. Your response, at these moments, lets them know whether you care about their needs getting met as much as you care about meeting your own. If you attempt to force them to do what you want—through guilt, blame, shame, or punishment—you demonstrate that you care mostly or only about your needs and that you are willing to use your immense power over them to get what you want.

Punishing students—whether with a look, a moralistic judgment intended to induce guilt, or with physical punishment—gives them the message that they are "wrong" or "bad," and that they deserve to suffer.

Deciding not to use punitive force over students does not mean that you have to give up your needs. In a relationship based classroom, each person's needs are taken into consideration with the intent to find strategies that will meet needs for everyone.

There are times when force is needed to protect people or things. For instance, if one student is about to hit another student, a teacher may need to hold one of them to prevent injury. In this case, force is used for the purpose of *protecting*, not punishing.

3. Student-Student Relationships

In a relationship based classroom the teacher is not the only person responsible for the learning environment. Teachers provide students with opportunities to learn new ways to express themselves, to listen to others, and to work interdependently, so that they become primary contributors to the cohesiveness and the vitality of the classroom.

The kinds of relationships that a teacher nurtures between and among students are a matter of intention. The underlying question is, *What kinds of relationships do you want to nurture in your classroom?* Once your intention is clear, it is possible to find and create ways to carry it out.

For mutually supportive interactions as well as compassion to flower, teachers in relationship based classrooms *act together* with students to meet the needs of individuals and the group. Mary Parker Follett, writing in the early twentieth century, called this capacity to act together to fulfill the most basic needs *power with* or *co-active power,* as contrasted with *power over* or *coercive power.*[2] She asserted that both our individual and group power increases when we act together. Another social scientist, Janet Surrey, describes *power with* as a developing human capacity to engage in a *mutually empathic relational process*[3]—a phrase that aptly describes the process of Nonviolent Communication. To describe power sharing, Marshall Rosenberg uses the term *life-enriching human connections,*[4] and Riane Eisler talks about *partnership* interactions in her book *Tomorrow's Children: A Blueprint for Partnership Education in the 21st Century.*[5]

Whatever label we use, we all have felt the exhilaration that arises when we work or play with another cooperatively, harmoniously, and both get our needs met. Imagine what could happen in a classroom if learners routinely experienced that kind of synergy or teamwork. Their needs for connection, collaboration, mutual contribution, productivity, and successful learning would be met. And, individual contributions to a synergistic group environment would have unimaginable effects, which could prove that the whole is definitely more than the sum of its parts.

From our own classroom experience and from teachers who have taken time to nurture partnership relationships in their classrooms, we know that it is surprisingly "natural" for students to work together cooperatively. When they have new choices and skills for how to interact, when their concerns are heard, and when their needs are being met, they find that working *with* one another is the most enjoyable way of being together. It does, however, take time to develop new skills and to unlearn old habits of comparing, judging, demanding, and coercing. Marianne Gothlin, a teacher at Skarpnacks Free School in Sweden, shared her observation that at Skarpnacks, which is based on NVC, there is an awareness among students that life at school is more fun if everyone is pleased.[6]

If you want to nurture partnership relationships in your classroom, you may find it helpful to notice the following:

> Classrooms should be places in which students can legitimately act on a rich variety of purposes, in which wonder and curiosity are alive, in which students and teachers live together and grow.
>
> *Nel Noddings*

How Do Your Students Share Their Gifts With One Another?

Each of us has gifts to bring to the classroom. In a relationship based classroom students are helped to recognize their gifts and the gifts that others have. They look for ways to give their gifts and receive the gifts of others to meet mutual needs.

At Skarpnacks Free School, students and teachers meet weekly, in groups of twenty to thirty, to talk about what contributed to satisfying their needs during the week and what didn't. Often it is small things that are appreciated, such as one girl sharing with another: "When you asked me to sit beside you yesterday at lunch I felt happy. I like it when someone enjoys having me around."[7]

How Do Your Students Communicate Their Feelings and Needs?

Do students recognize their own feelings and the needs that motivate their actions?

Do students recognize the feelings and needs of others?

Are they able and willing to talk about their feelings and needs?

Are they able and willing to listen for the feelings and needs of others?

Are they able to find mutually satisfying ways to meet needs?

(Communicating feelings and needs is at the heart of NVC and is explained in Chapter 4.)

When academic culture dismisses inner truth and honors only the external world, students as well as teachers lose heart.

Parker Palmer

Do Students Make Requests of Others or Do They Make Demands?

When people hear a demand they usually do not want to give what is asked for because their needs for autonomy and giving freely are not being met. Learning to make requests of others rather than demands makes joyful giving and receiving possible.

(Making requests is an essential component of NVC and is explained in Chapter 4.)

How Often Do Your Students Make Decisions About Their Learning and Life in the Classroom?

According to Alfie Kohn:

> There are few educational contrasts so sharp and meaningful as that between students being told what the teacher expects of them, what they are and are not permitted to do, and students coming together to reflect on how they can live and learn together. It is the difference between being prepared to spend a lifetime doing what one is told and being prepared to take an active role in a democratic society.[8]

When students are involved in making decisions about classroom life, they feel engaged, interested, empowered, and hopeful. The more decisions students make, the more this is so, since many needs are met for them:

participation, inclusion, respect, consideration, trust, power over their environment and their learning.

(For ideas about how students can make class agreements, see Chapter 5, Daily Giraffe: Co-creating Ground Rules.)

To What Extent Do Students Learn Together and From Each Other?

It is not considered cheating to solve problems together in a non-competitive, relationship based classroom. A team approach to learning is encouraged; however, there is also ample opportunity for those who want to study on their own to do so. What is most important is that students have many successful learning experiences every day of their school lives.

Do Your Students Have Forums to Express Themselves and to Hear Others?

Students need a variety of forums to:

Share what is happening in their lives

Talk about their concerns about world events

Respond and react to what they are learning

Discuss how the classroom is functioning

Share appreciation

Solve problems

Make decisions together

Plan activities and events

Resolve conflicts

Having a variety of forums for students to use for meeting together encourages and enriches student-student relationships. Nonviolent Communication helps make these meetings productive and satisfying.

The following are suggestions for student forums:

Council

Meeting in a circle, in *Council*, is used in cultures throughout the world and satisfies needs for inclusion, equality, and connection, as well as giving practice in group listening. It also allows everyone's voice to be heard.

(For more about Council, see Chapter 5, Daily Giraffe: Council.)

Class Discussions

Taking turns leading class discussions allows students to see different perspectives and to gain facilitating skills. So that more students can talk and be heard, it is often helpful to divide the group into small groups. While these discussions may seem chaotic to teachers, they can be valuable for students, allowing them to express honestly, to listen carefully, and to learn how to give and receive within the group. We have seen a great deal of value in the struggle to learn these skills.

Dyads

Talking in pairs gives everyone an opportunity to talk and be heard. When students meet one to one and hear how life is that day for one other person in the class, understanding and compassion gradually begin to grow. Rotating students so that they hear the daily concerns of every other student in the class dissolves enemy images as they gradually realize how similar their concerns are.

Role-plays

Role-plays can be fun. They are also powerful ways to step inside another's shoes. They offer practice for both expressing and listening from the heart.

(See Chapter 5, Daily Giraffe: Role-plays.)

Empathy Buddies & Empaths on Duty

Having empathy buddies can increase connection between students and give opportunities to practice empathy skills. Students can volunteer to be an Empath on Duty in the classroom and/or on the playground. Throughout the day, students can go to these people when they want or need someone to listen to them.

(Read more about Empathy in Chapter 4.)

A point well worth remembering is that a "safe" classroom environment is one where it is OK to fail.

Esther Wright

Third-Siders

Third-Siders help resolve differences between two students who are having a conflict. Even young students can learn skills to mediate conflicts among peers. These coaches help identify the facts of an event, the feelings, the needs, and the requests of each person. The Third-Sider facilitates a flow of empathy between the two parties so that they can reach mutually satisfying resolutions.

(See Chapter 5, Daily Giraffe: Resolving Conflicts.)

4. Student-Learning Relationship

When students are aware of their own learning processes and have many opportunities to make connections with the world, they are on their way to becoming confident, life-long learners.

Forming a Relationship to One's Own Learning Process

Each of us has our own learning process. We each have things that spark our interest and whet our appetite for learning. We have questions we like to ask and ways we like to find answers. Becoming aware of how we learn and knowing what we care to learn about are perhaps the most important parts of the learning process. Learning about ourselves as learners is a vital component of a relationship based classroom. We find it helpful for teachers to notice the following:

Do Your Students Know What Their Interests, Talents, and Learning Styles Are?

Are students curious? What stimulates their sense of wonder? Do they know what their interests are? Are they aware of their talents and gifts? Do they know how they learn best?

Are Your Students Actively Engaged in Learning?

How much time do students spend discovering, exploring, experimenting? How much time do they spend listening to teachers, reading assigned material, completing worksheets? Are they curious, eager, excited, and playfully engaged in learning at school, or do they seem to be "doing time"?

Are Your Students Involved in Setting Learning Objectives?

In a relationship based classroom, students and teachers work together to set learning objectives, based on what the student is eager to learn *and* what the teacher sees as valuable for the student to learn. Objectives are determined, assessed, and revised through ongoing dialogue between teacher and student. Students can also help each other decide upon objectives and the strategies that are likely to meet them.

When learning objectives are determined outside the classroom, as in the case of standardized testing, students and teachers often experience doubt, anxiety, and resistance. They need empathy for the loss of autonomy that they experience. They may also need to talk about how these external objectives do or do not have meaning or value for them. Teachers and students can explore what needs could be met by working toward required objectives.

Are Your Students Involved in Evaluating Their Learning?

Learning to assess one's own progress—evaluating accurately how well we have met our objectives and fulfilled our needs—is a vital skill to develop.

The following example illustrates how students can evaluate their work in terms of their own desires and goals rather than in terms of comparison with others.

A girl at Skarpnacks Free School was not pleased with the results of a math test she took the day before. She brought it up in class:

Student: I feel sad and uncomfortable with my results.

Teacher: Can you clarify what makes you feel sad and uncomfortable?

Student: Yes, I wish I had made other priorities.... I have not put much attention to math lately. I understand that I need to have more patience with myself to learn this.[9]

Do Your Evaluations of Students' Work Contribute to Their Learning Process?

We have observed that when teachers use static language—right/wrong, correct/incorrect, good/bad, acceptable/unacceptable—to evaluate students' work, students learn to work for teachers' approval rather than working to learn for themselves. This kind of evaluation also undermines safety in a classroom; students become afraid to experiment and try new things. A student's learning process suffers on both counts.

Using a process language like NVC rather than static evaluations makes a connection with students and provides them with helpful feedback. In the following examples of process evaluations, the teacher honestly shares her reactions and engages with the student's learning process.

A teacher, talking with a student, says: "I'm puzzled about why this character in your story is feeling so sad. Can you help me understand what is going on with him?"

Looking at a math problem, a teacher says: "On this problem, I see I got a different answer than you did. I'm confused. I'd like to understand how you got the answer you did. Would you be willing to show me?"[10]

How Do Your Students Relate to Mistakes and/or Failure?

When students are judged, graded, and ridiculed for failures and mistakes, they usually do not feel safe enough to risk trying something new. Mistakes and failures, as viewed in many traditional classrooms, can stop learners in their tracks. They often feel embarrassed, discouraged, or ashamed, thinking that they shouldn't be making mistakes and that something's wrong with them. Their learning process suffers from such self-criticism, and they are liable to shut down and miss the valuable learning that is possible when things don't turn out the way they had hoped. We can help students learn to take mistakes and failures in stride and to mine them for information that allows them to take their next steps in the learning process rather than get bogged down in self-doubt and discouragement. We can contribute to a balanced perspective by noticing and helping students learn from successes, too.

(See Chapter 3, Premise 4.)

Forming a Relationship to the World Through a Curriculum

As has been observed by J. Krishnamurti, William Glasser, and others,[11] students are most likely to be responsive to a curriculum that is responsive to them—one that encourages them to recognize that *they* are a part of the interconnectedness of all things and not just observers studying interconnectedness. In looking at curriculum, it helps to notice the following:

Curriculum is about relationship: the interconnectedness of everything.

Sarah Pirtle

What Is the Curriculum Frame That You Hold or That You Have to Negotiate?

The curriculum is a frame on the world that a teacher holds and within which students make mental, and sometimes physical, forays into the world of people, events, thoughts, philosophies, arts, and cultures. The curriculum reflects the purpose of education that the people who wrote it have in mind. What purpose did the people who wrote your curriculum have in mind? Does it suit your needs and those of your students? What would you add to it or subtract from it? How can you work with your curriculum in a way that is the most meaningful to you?

How Often Do You Focus on the Interplay of Feelings and Needs in Your Curriculum—Especially in Literature, History, and the Sciences?

A relationship based classroom, with its focus on honoring feelings and meeting individual and group needs, is a microcosm of what tribes and nations have tried to do throughout history—to meet needs in the best way that they could. This microcosm can provide insight for lively learning about the macrocosm. The sciences can be seen from the perspective of successive advances in meeting human needs for shelter, food, protection, communication, transportation, relaxation, etc. History can be seen as the study of the strategies that different groups of people have used to meet their basic human needs. Literature can be looked at as the interplay of needs of a wide range of individuals and the results of the strategies that they chose to meet their needs.

To What Extent Is the Study of Human Life Connected to the Community, to All Other Life Forms, the Biosphere, and the Planet?

Is your curriculum actually about the interconnectedness of everything? Does it acknowledge and respect the layers and networks of interdependence that make human life not only possible but diverse, awe inspiring, and meaningful? Like the classroom, the community that the students live in has its own needs. Each life form has its needs, so does the biosphere and the planet. What kinds of needs might the biosphere and the planet have?

When students feel supported and successful in the classroom, they rarely act out. When teachers feel supported and successful in their school, they rarely burn out.

Esther Wright

Do Students Make Meaningful Connections With the Curriculum?

Is the curriculum in some way relevant to the interests, passions, and lives of your students? If it is, they are likely to participate eagerly. If it isn't, they are likely to find something else to connect with during their hours at school. As the holders of the curriculum frame, teachers need to be able to answer one question that students frequently ask: Why do we have to study history, math, writing, etc.? This can be a difficult question to answer, and students know when we are giving them canned answers. It's a fair question, and a teacher's willingness to address it can go a long way to create trust and openness in future communications. Why do you think that your students have to study history, science, math, etc.?

(For examples of curricula that have a large frame, see Resources.)

How Many Resources Are in the Classroom and How Accessible to Students Are They?

How we learn is as important as what we learn. Students might not be as upset with the subjects that they are asked to study as they are with how the subjects are presented. How many resources are available to students besides the teacher? Perhaps there are reference books available. How many resources are available in addition to books? Students with varying modalities for processing information and varying learning styles need different avenues for making connections with the material that they are studying.[12] Are students encouraged to think of the wider community as a learning resource, and do they have easy access to it?

Summary

There are three questions that can be useful to a teacher who wants to establish a relationship based classroom: Am I creating safety and trust? Am I taking my needs and the students' needs into consideration? Am I using communication that facilitates respectful, meaningful dialogue?

We hope that the suggestions and questions in this section contribute to meeting your students' needs for safety and trust and your needs for inspiration, encouragement, and support.

Section II

Tools for Creating the Compassionate Classroom

Introduction to Section II

In Section I we established two primary ways for creating safety and trust in the classroom—focusing on needs and learning a language of giving and receiving. In Section II we offer tools for doing this.

The Five Premises in Chapter 3 provide insight into needs—how to understand, identify, and meet them. These Premises are reminders of our human capacities for empathy and caring. The exercises in each Premise can be used as tools for both teachers and students to establish safe ground for joyful learning and compassion. Chapter 4 is a step-by-step description of Nonviolent Communication, a mutually respectful language of giving and receiving. This language connects minds and hearts and attunes them to what we have in common as human beings. Practicing this language integrates our thinking, expands our range of choices for compassionate interactions, and generates well-being by helping us meet our needs. This is illustrated in the four dialogues at the end of the chapter. Chapter 5 provides activities and games for learning and practicing NVC and completes our toolkit for creating and sustaining a compassionate classroom.

Chapter 3
Rediscover Your Giving and Receiving Nature

A capacity to care is the thing which gives life its deepest meaning and significance.

Pablo Casals

The ways that we think, talk, and interact with others are based on what we hold to be true about human nature. If we believe that our nature is primarily aggressive, selfish, competitive, and egocentric, our thoughts and actions reflect those beliefs. The following Five Premises are reminders of what we, the authors, believe is our compassionate nature. These Premises have the potential to engender a change of heart for those who live by them. This change of heart can be the source of more learning and less conflict in the classroom. In this chapter we share our understanding of the Premises with examples, exercises, and group activities.

We hope that you will explore these Premises by doing the exercises yourself. Based on your own experience with them, you can choose which exercises you want to share with your students and how you want to share them. We encourage you to modify the exercises and group activities to suit your needs and the needs of your students.

An Overview of the Five Premises and the Main Points of Each

Premise 1:

We are all natural givers.

- We each have a lot to give.
- We enjoy giving when we do it willingly.

Premise 2:

We can give and receive to meet the most needs for everyone.

- Needs are universal and identifiable.
- Our needs are independent of specific people.
- We are always trying to meet our needs.
- Feelings are helpful messengers of met and unmet needs.
- Identifying our needs is empowering.

Premise 3:

To meet needs we can become more choiceful about how we think, listen, talk, and act.

- We are agents of choice.
- There are many ways to meet needs.
- We can choose how we act.
- We can choose how we think.
- We can choose how we listen.
- We can choose how we talk.

Premise 4:

We can continually learn new ways to meet needs.

- We can refine strategies to meet needs.
- We can celebrate when strategies work.
- We can learn from strategies that don't work.

Premise 5:

By focusing on needs we can prevent, reduce, and resolve conflicts.

- Needs are never in conflict.
- Conflicts occur when we think there is only one way or one person to meet a need.
- Conflicts occur when a strategy chosen to meet a need means that some other important needs will not get met.
- For the most fun, we can find ways to meet everyone's needs.

Premise 1: We Are All Natural Givers

Giving implies to make the other person a giver also,
and they both share in the joy of what they have brought to life.
In the act of giving lies the expression of my aliveness.

— Erich Fromm

A parent gets up in the early hours of the morning to feed the new baby.

A child rushes home from school with a colorfully wrapped plaster of Paris hand print that she has made and excitedly places it on her dad's favorite chair.

Members of a Florida community work together to help each other clean up their devastated homes after a hurricane.

These are ways of giving that well up in people spontaneously out of the desire to contribute to the well-being of others. In fact, it is this desire to contribute to the lives of others that typifies human nature.[1]

Because we live in families, neighborhoods, and towns, our lives are interwoven with the lives of many others. Rather than separate islands of self-sufficiency, we are interdependent members of social groups. Membership in the group is enhanced by sharing our gifts and our bounty with others.

We each have a lot to give.

Each of us possesses a wealth of ideas, talents, skills, and the fruits of our interests that we can share with others. Some people give their singing, some give vegetables from their garden, some give cookies, some give poems or paintings.

Even if all personal skills and talents were set aside, there are some things that we all can give: time, energy, attention. Sometimes just sitting in the same room with someone who is ill is helpful, so sharing time can be a gift. When a family member has a big job to do, sharing energy can be a gift. When a friend is in distress, our attention can be a gift.

If, as a society, we want to raise caring adults, it will be important to provide opportunities for young people to find out what their gifts are and to experience themselves as givers—active, aware givers.

We will also want our children to practice being receivers—active, aware receivers. Willingness to receive from another is an additional gift that we all have to give. Receiving a gift with genuine acknowledgment and appreciation for the giver generates a flow of goodwill. The result is that each person is an equal partner in a dance of mutual giving.

Exercise:

Think of ways you give from the heart. Make a list of ways or things you can give.

Make a list of things you receive from others.

Group Activity:

Make a resource book of gifts each person in the classroom/school wants to offer others.

We enjoy giving when we do it willingly.

When we hear another's needs and realize how we can contribute to helping her fulfill them, we often feel an impulse to give that is akin to the parent feeding the child or the neighbors helping one another clean up after the hurricane. We experience a rush of pleasure that comes from giving freely with no expectation of getting anything back. Empathy for the feelings and needs of another is a heartfelt connection that allows the spirit of giving to flow through us.

Domination or compulsion of any kind is a direct hindrance to freedom and intelligence.

J. Krishnamurti

While we are always receiving at the same time that we are giving, if we set out only "to get" by giving, a heartfelt connection is less possible. Also, if there is the sense of obligation that one *must* give, *ought to* give, or *should* give, the flow of heartfelt connection is interrupted.

Exercise:

Think of a specific time you gave to someone just because you wanted to.

- What did you give?
- How did you feel?
- What motivated you to give?

Group Activity:

Draw a picture of the above giving event and show how you felt about it.

- Share your pictures with one another.
- Notice all the different ways to give.
- Notice how you feel when you give just because you want to give.

Premise 2: We Can Give and Receive to Meet the Most Needs for Everyone

I believe it is our nature to enjoy giving and receiving in a compassionate manner.

— Marshall Rosenberg

As strange as it may sound, we give our gifts to meet our own needs. Among these needs is the need to contribute to the well-being of others. To fully embrace our giving and receiving nature, an understanding of needs and a vocabulary to express them is essential.

Needs are universal and identifiable.

Needs refer to what sustains us physically, emotionally, mentally, socially, and spiritually. Needs motivate action. Human beings share basic survival needs that include: air, water, food, rest, and safety. In addition to these basics, we also need love, learning, friends, fun, and some degree of autonomy. Since people everywhere have the same needs, it is possible to understand what motivates people, even when life-styles, beliefs, and languages are very different, and *even when we disagree with their actions.*

Our needs are independent of specific people.

Needs are most clearly expressed in three words, for example: "I need clarity"; "I need knowledge"; "I need companionship." We might have a specific person in mind to help us meet a need; however, to have a need met we are not dependent upon that one person. Needs do not include specific people or specific actions, as in: "I need you to...." Thinking that only one person or action can meet a need is a primary source of conflict, a point which will be developed more in Premise 5.

Exercise:

Make a list of universal needs that you and all people have. (For ideas, you can refer to the Needs List in Chapter 4.)

We are always trying to meet our needs.

When we see the children sleeping, we know that
they are meeting their need for rest after
a full day of learning and play.

When we see our neighbor jogging every morning,
we can see that as a way for him to meet his need
for health and exercise.

When a student spends long hours studying,
we can guess that she is meeting her need for learning.

When a friend tells us a joke, she is probably attempting
to meet her needs for humor and playful interaction or
perhaps relief from pain.

When we call a friend to tell him about something
that worries us, we might be trying to meet needs
for empathy and understanding.

In fact, whatever we do, it is an attempt to meet one or more of our human needs.

Exercise:

Think of something you did this morning.

- What need were you trying to meet?
- Can you think of other needs you were meeting?
- Think of something else you said or did and identify the need(s) you were trying to meet.
- Can you think of anything you have said or done that was not an attempt to meet a need?

A need is life seeking expression.

Marshall Rosenberg

Feelings are helpful messengers of met and unmet needs.

Our feelings are important messengers, telling us when our needs are fulfilled and when they are not. Pleasurable feelings such as *happy, satisfied,* and *joyful* give us the message that our needs are being met. Painful feelings like *sad, upset,* and *frustrated* give the message that our needs are not being met. When we pay attention to our feelings and listen to their messages, we get important clues about how to meet our own needs. When we pay attention to the feelings of other people and listen to the messages they give, we get important clues about what they value and what they need.

Exercise:

Think of a time when you felt very satisfied.

- What need was being met?

Think of a time when you felt frustrated or disappointed.

- What need was not met?

Group Activity:

Make a chart or a collage of Feelings When Needs Are Met and another for Feelings When Needs Are Not Met. Add to it as you hear or think of more feeling words. (For suggestions, refer to the List of Feeling Words in Chapter 4.)

Identifying our needs is empowering.

Identifying our needs empowers us to take action in our own behalf. The more accurately we identify them, the more likely it is that we will take effective action. Conversely, if we don't identify what we need, we are likely to act in ways that are unsatisfying and even regrettable. For example, if I feel irritable and tired at the end of a school day and I recognize that I haven't eaten anything since breakfast, I can see that my need is for nutrition. With this need clearly in mind, I'll be most likely to prepare something that will be nourishing. However, if I feel irritable and tired and don't look for the cause of those feelings (my body's need for nutrition), I might grab a candy bar or yell at someone.

Unfortunately, at present, thinking in terms of feelings and needs is uncommon. Few of us have a vocabulary of feelings that extends beyond *mad, sad, glad,* and *frustrated,* and many of us have been taught that having needs reflects badly on our character because it shows that we are "selfish" or "needy." The belief seems to be that a *strong* person doesn't need anything and a *good* person puts his or her needs last.

Creating a society of people who don't know that they have needs, who believe that it is unacceptable to have needs, and who have a limited vocabulary for talking about feelings and needs has unfortunate and often tragic consequences. People who are unaware of their needs often act in ineffective and even destructive ways. Those who fill our prisons because they have hurt or killed another human being were not aware of the *real* human needs they were trying to meet when they acted as they did. As a result, they weren't able to consider ways to act that would have truly served them and the other person. People who take harmful drugs usually aren't aware of the real need(s) they are trying to satisfy. If they knew that what they really wanted was relaxation and relief, peace of mind, or belonging, it's more likely they would be able to think of other ways to meet those specific needs that are not as costly to their health and well- being as drugs are. In the classroom we have seen many students hit others or say hurtful things out of anger and lack of awareness of their own needs. Things changed when they learned to identify needs for respect and consideration, and when they learned a way to express what they *really* wanted.

For example: A teacher says to a student, "I think you're just being lazy by not finishing that work." The child replies, "You're mean!" This defensive response is the only way this child has learned to deal with the pain of unmet needs for respect and understanding. His response is not likely to meet his needs; in fact, the teacher may give him a trip to the principal's office or something else that adds to his pain. If, instead of name calling, the child has learned to identify his needs for understanding and respect, he will probably find ways to respond that are much more satisfying to him and to the teacher.

If, in the first place, the teacher had been aware of his own needs—perhaps to understand what is really going on with this student—he could have expressed his feelings and needs something like this:

> "When I see that your project isn't finished on the day you said it would be, and I see you working on something else, I'm puzzled. I would like to understand what stopped you from completing your first project?"

When teachers learn to identify their own needs, they are empowered to act in ways that are satisfying to them. When teachers learn to identify the needs of their students, they are empowered to contribute to their well-being. And, whether teachers realize it or not, the behavior that they model to students is the behavior that students model in relationship to each other. The result is that when teachers pay attention to the needs of students, students start paying attention to the needs of one another, and this is the beginning of a truly cooperative, compassionate learning environment.

If an entire society of people learned to pay attention to their own needs as well as the needs of others, we would be on our way to creating a world that has the potential to work for everyone.

Exercise:

Think of a time when you knew what you needed and chose to do something to meet that need.

- What was the need?
- What did you do to help meet your need?
- How did you feel?

Exercise:

Think of a time when someone told you what would help them meet their need and you were willing and able to help.

- What was their need?
- What did you give to help meet their need?
- How did you feel?
- What needs of yours were met?

Premise 3:
To Meet Needs We Can Become More Choiceful About How We Think, Listen, Talk, and Act

Out beyond ideas of wrongdoing and rightdoing,
there is a field. I'll meet you there.
— Rumi

Whether we are aware of it or not, we have a range of choices about how we think, talk, listen, and act. When we are conscious of these choices we can take actions that will be satisfying.

We are agents of choice.

We are agents of choice from the time we are born; however, in our culture, the opportunities to make our own choices typically increase with age and experience. When we are young, adults make most of the decisions about our lives. In order for us to grow into adults who are able to make responsible decisions for ourselves, we need many more opportunities at young ages to make choices about our own lives.

Exercise:

Make a list of things that others (family, community, government) choose for you.

Make a list of choices you make for yourself.

Group Activity:

Ask everyone in the class to make the two lists from the previous page, and then share them with one another. What do you notice? Find out what students notice.

Note: Young people may feel irritated or angry hearing adults talk about making choices and taking responsibility for needs. They know that parents, teachers, and other adults make most of their decisions for them and their choices often seem limited to just two—to comply or to rebel. Most children live in the midst of a seemingly endless number of rules and expectations that often don't make sense to them; they might not believe that they have any control over meeting their own needs. They need and want more opportunities to make choices about their lives. They also need a great deal of empathy for the gap between the autonomy they would like to have and the limited number of choices adults offer them.

Freedom is the capacity to pause between stimulus and response.

Rollo May

There are many ways to meet needs.

We live in a world of abundance. For every need, there are many ways or strategies to fulfill it. Painting, sculpting, dancing, singing are different ways to meet a need for creative expression. To meet a need for learning, we can read, watch movies, listen to tapes, discuss with others, or think quietly. If it is friendship we want, there are many ways to meet that need as well.

Exercise:

Think of a specific need: play, respect, safety, learning, and so on, and list different ways that you have found to satisfy it.

Group Activity:

Everyone in the group makes a list of ways they have met a specific need (the same need for everyone). Share the lists with one another. Discuss the results of the various strategies.

Exercise:

Think of a time when a need of yours was not met.

- What need were you trying to meet?

- What strategy did you use to meet it?

- Can you think of a different strategy that might have worked better?

We can choose how we act.

I can always choose how I act. When my intention is to engage fully in giving and receiving, I will be more likely to choose actions that contribute to meeting the most needs for everyone.

We can choose how we think.

As well as choosing my actions, I can choose where I put my focus. If I focus on thoughts of who's right and who's wrong, what's fair and what's not, who's bad and who's good, I will spend my time analyzing, judging, blaming and criticizing—ways of thinking that make life less harmonious and distract attention from meeting needs. When I think that others are *manipulating* me, *taking advantage* of me, *ignoring* me, *disrespecting* me, I will likely feel annoyed, irritated, or angry. If, instead, I think in terms of the needs people are trying to meet in every action they take, I am more likely to feel compassion.

We can choose how we listen.

I always have a choice about how I listen and what I listen for. When someone is upset and is not expressing feelings and needs but is using language that sounds like criticism or blame, I can choose how and what I hear. If I interpret what they are saying as an attack on me, I will react defensively, out of hurt, fear, or anger. Whenever I listen to my own or another person's interpretation, criticism, and/or blame, with my ears tuned to who's right and who's wrong, I spend much of my time stressed, irritated, and generally upset.

When, instead, I choose to listen with my ears tuned to feelings and needs, no matter what a person is saying or how he is saying it, I am immediately reconnected to my giving and receiving nature.

We can choose how we talk.

I always have a choice about how I talk. Talking is a way to connect with others and to communicate—share information and experiences, solve problems, and explore ideas. When I think and hear in terms of judgment and blame, my talk will tend to reflect that thinking. My conversation will be about who's right, who's wrong, who's to blame, and who should do what. My analysis, judgment, and blame make it hard to hear the heart song that is really being sung.

Instead, I can choose a way to talk that expresses the heart of human concern. I can share information about how I experience the world in terms of my feelings and needs, and what would make life more wonderful for me. When we exchange this kind of information, we play together in the field that the mystic poet Rumi describes:

Out beyond ideas of wrongdoing and rightdoing
there is a field. I'll meet you there.
When the soul lies down in that grass,
the world is too full to talk about.
Ideas, language, even the phrase "each other"
doesn't make any sense.

Premise 4:
We Can Continually Learn New Ways to Meet Needs

Everything is in a constant process of discovery and creating. Life is intent on finding what works, not what's "right."

— Margaret Wheatley

When we know ourselves to be connected to all others, acting compassionately is simply the natural thing to do.

Rachel Naomi Remen

Meeting needs is the number one activity of life, in or out of the classroom. There are hundreds of opportunities each day to practice and to refine our skills as teachers and to help students refine their skills. With a few pointers and a little practice and patience with ourselves and our students, it is possible to continually create, invent, and intuit new ways to meet needs.

Even very young children can take responsibility for meeting their own needs. Victoria shared Nonviolent Communication skills with a kindergarten classroom and several parents remarked at how surprised and happy they were to hear their children shift from whining and arguing to brainstorming strategies for meeting their own needs. Some parents even reported hearing their children brainstorm need-meeting strategies with siblings and friends.

We can refine strategies to meet needs.

When a need has been recognized, it is possible to brainstorm many different strategies to fulfill it. For example, if I'm feeling distressed every day when I hear my students arguing, I might realize that my needs are for more harmony, cooperation, and tranquillity. With these needs in mind, I think of possible strategies to fulfill them. One strategy might be to talk with my students about their behavior and my distress. Another strategy might be to talk with other teachers about what they do to encourage harmony among their students. Still another strategy might be to start an NVC program in the classroom.

Let's say that I chose to talk with my students about my distress, and in spite of my efforts I was not able to convey my need in a way that resulted in the harmony and cooperation that I had hoped for. Since my needs are not being met, I have the choice to refine the present strategy or try another one. Because I know that there are many ways to meet needs, I can continue to refine strategies until I'm successful. There is no attempt to judge myself harshly and no expectation that I get it "right" the first, second, or even third time that I try. When I move slowly and *take time* to notice whether or not needs are being met, I am able to refine and change strategies as I go.

Steps for Taking Responsibility for Our Own Needs

1) Identify the need

2) Choose a strategy for meeting the need

3) Try out the strategy

4) Evaluate the strategy

5) Refine the strategy or try another one

We can celebrate when strategies work.

When our strategies work and needs are met, we know more about how to take care of ourselves, and we are able to proceed with more confidence in our ability to find additional strategies that sustain us. This is a time for celebration.

We can learn from strategies that don't work.

When strategies don't meet needs, it is tempting for some people to label them as "mistakes," and to be drawn into a downward spiral of self-criticism, self-doubt, and self-punishment. In fact, a mistake is simply a strategy for meeting a need that didn't work out the way we hoped it would. Instead of playing a self-blame game and judging our mistakes as bad, we can reconnect with our feelings and needs and find out how to tinker with, tweak, or otherwise adjust our strategies for more satisfying results.

It can help to remember that *we are always doing the best we can* to meet our needs. If we are afraid of making mistakes, we will miss opportunities to try new things. We won't feel free to explore, experiment, and play. Rather than blame and judge ourselves for making a mistake, it can be helpful to mourn the mistake and to learn from it.

To learn from mistakes, I can:

Observe: What did I do or say that I regret?

Notice: What am I telling myself about what I did?

Am I judging myself?

Ask: What needs was I trying to meet?

Ask: What needs did I meet?

Ask: How could I have met those needs more effectively?

Request: What do I want to do now to meet my needs?

Exercise:

Think of a mistake you made—
something you wish you had done differently.

- What did you do, or what didn't you do, that you regret?

- What did you tell yourself about what you did or didn't do?

- How do you feel about it now?

- What needs were you trying to meet? How do you think you could have met those needs more effectively?

- Is there anything you want to do now to meet those needs?

Premise 5:
By Focusing on Needs We Can Prevent, Reduce, and Resolve Conflicts

The whole idea of compassion is based on a keen awareness of the interdependence of all living things.

— Thomas Merton

- **Needs are never in conflict.**
- **Conflicts occur when we think there is only one way to meet a need.**
- **Conflicts occur when a strategy chosen to meet a need means that some other important needs will not get met.**

Most often, people experience conflict as painful and want to find ways to prevent, reduce, and resolve it. This can be done by identifying needs and choosing strategies to meet them that work for everyone. At the level of needs there are no conflicts; there are only our human needs. For example, there are my needs for learning and connection and your needs for learning and connection; there are my needs for trust and respect and your needs for trust and respect. These are facts about each of us.

If needs are not the source of conflict, what is? Conflicts occur when we think that there is only one way or one person to meet a need. Conflicts also occur when the strategy chosen to meet a need means that some other important needs will not get met—mine or yours.

The following example illustrates both of these sources of conflict. Imagine that something happens in a classroom and the teacher wants to talk, as soon as possible, with the parents of one of her students. To meet her need to communicate with the parents, she decides to have her students write a twenty-minute essay while she makes a telephone call. However, the students have just finished a long math period and are tired and want free time. Believing that there is only one way to meet her need, the teacher is unable to hear the feelings and needs of the students. She keeps trying new strategies to convince them that she is right and that they "should" write the essay.

She uses language that triggers guilt in the students, such as, "Yesterday after math I did something that you wanted to do; today it's your turn to do something that I want you to do." She tries labeling or name calling and says, "I don't think that you're tired; I think that you're lazy," which is likely to trigger resentment and irritation. She even tries threats, "If you don't write in class, I'll give you an 'F' for class participation, and you'll have to do the essay as homework tonight," which is likely to trigger anxiety and anger. In each case, because she is convinced that there is only one way to meet her need (writing an essay), a conflict is in the making.

By contrast, when a teacher steps back and focuses on the needs of her students as well as her own needs, she is likely to try some different strategies. She could ask the students if they would be willing to work quietly on a project of their own choice for twenty minutes. She could ask students to take turns reading a story to each other while she makes the phone call. Or, she could brainstorm with her students to find another solution that would meet everyone's needs. Any one of these strategies would be an attempt to meet the students' needs as well as her own and would be more likely to elicit cooperation.

At the level of needs, there is no conflict between the teacher's need for time to deal with an urgent issue and the students' need for consideration around their tiredness. It is at the level of strategies that conflict can easily occur.

Preventing, reducing, and resolving conflicts relies upon an ability to focus on needs and to be creative and flexible in determining strategies to meet needs.

Exercise:

Think of a time when you did something without regard for how your action affected someone else.

- What did you do?

- What was the result?

- What needs were met for you?

- What needs were not met for you?

- What needs were not met for the other person?

Exercise:

Think of a time when you gave up your needs.

- What did you do?

- What needs did you give up?

- How did you feel then?

- How do you feel now?

Group Activity:

Act out a skit of someone taking the ball from someone else at recess.

Discuss with students:

- In taking the ball, what needs was this person trying to meet?
- What happened after he took it? How did he feel?
- What needs of his were met? What needs were not met?
- How did the person who first had the ball feel?
- What needs were not met for that person?

Exercise:

Think of a time that a need of yours was not met.

- What need were you trying to meet?
- What strategy did you use to meet that need?
- Can you think of a different strategy that might have worked better?

For the most fun, we can find ways to meet everyone's needs.

Since there are many ways to meet needs, looking for ways to meet the most needs, our own and those of others, often brings to light new and even more fun and satisfying options.

Exercise:

Imagine that you have prepared a new unit of study for your class. You have spent a great deal of time creating activities that appeal to the various learning styles of your students.

- What images come to mind?
- What needs of yours do you hope to meet?
- What needs of your students do you hope to meet?
- What feelings do you have when you imagine students participating in this unit study?

Exercise:

Imagine a child bringing her dog to class for show and tell.

- What needs might she be meeting?
- What needs of the class might be met?
- What needs of the teacher?
- What needs of the dog might be met?
- What needs might not be met:

  For the students?

  For the teacher?

  For the dog?

Exercise:

Think of an especially happy time involving your class. List all the needs that were met for you and the others involved.

Each moment is an invitation to rediscover your giving and receiving nature.

- You are invited to see yourself as a giver—rich beyond measure with gifts that will help you meet your own needs and the needs of others.
- You are invited to see others as people doing the best they can to meet their needs.
- You are invited to see yourself as having choices about how you think, talk, listen, and how you act toward others.
- You are invited to tinker and try things, make mistakes, and learn new ways to give to yourself and others.

Family members, friends, colleagues, and perhaps especially students give you countless invitations to receive their gifts and to contribute your gifts to their lives. Imagine children coming to school every day inviting you to see their true nature. What a difference this kind of seeing would make in their willingness and desire to learn with and from you.

Perhaps the following song expresses how students would like you to see them.

A song to teach your students:

See Me Beautiful

by Red and Kathy Grammer

See me beautiful
Look for the best in me
It's what I really am
And all I want to be
It may take some time
It may be hard to find
But see me beautiful

See me beautiful
Each and every day
Could you take a chance
Could you find a way
To see me shining through
In everything I do
And see me beautiful?

From *Teaching Peace,* RedNote Records
With permission from Red and Kathy Grammer[2]

Chapter 4
Relearn the Language of Giving and Receiving

> The life force for humankind is, perhaps, nothing more or less than the passionate energy to connect, express, and communicate.
>
> *Rosamund Zander*

The Language of Giving and Receiving is our natural language: it speaks of our common human needs and what would make life more wonderful for us. This way of communicating makes it easy to give to one another and to receive from one another—to enjoy and enrich life.

Jackal Language

Unfortunately, this is not the language most of us learned. For thousands of years we have been speaking a language that actually makes it difficult for people to give and receive joyfully. It is a language that meets only some needs and that contributes to a tremendous amount of pain in the world, including conflicts that arise every day in classrooms.

This language has the following characteristics:

It labels people: *You're mean. . . . She's bossy. . . . He's dumb. . . . I'm lazy. . . .*

It judges: *I'm right. . . . You're wrong. . . . We're good. . . . They're bad.*

It blames: *It's her fault. . . . You should have. . . . I'm to blame. . . .*

It denies choice: *You have to. . . . I can't. . . . They made me. . . .*

It makes demands: *If you don't do what I want, you'll be sorry.*

For fun, we call this language Jackal Language because (metaphorically) the jackal is low to the ground, and its sight is limited to what is right in front of it. People using Jackal Language don't see that they have choices and often only know one way to process their experiences—by going into their heads where they think about who's good, who's bad, who's right, who's wrong, and who's to blame. Jackal Language doesn't have a vocabulary of feelings and needs; an inner life is hardly recognized and is rarely expressed. This language conveys only thoughts, beliefs, and opinions. Instead of allowing us to play a game of Giving and Receiving, Jackal Language perpetuates a game of Naming and Blaming.

Our language habits are at the core of how we imagine the world.

Neil Postman

With all the criticizing, labeling, blaming, and demanding, Jackal Language is not very much fun; yet for many of us, it is all that we know. Over time Jackal Language has become so automatic that we find ourselves communicating in this way before we know what is happening. We do this even when we see, time and again, that using Jackal Language doesn't get us what we want and even aggravates the situation.

Fortunately, more and more people are rediscovering and relearning a language of giving and receiving. With this language, destructive, life-alienating jackal messages can be translated into life-serving messages—messages that contribute to meeting needs.

The language of giving and receiving has many names, including: Nonviolent Communication, Compassionate Communication, and the Language of the Heart. For fun, it is also called Giraffe Language.*

* Note: Nonviolent Communication is sometimes called Giraffe Language. CNVC's use of the image and term *Giraffe* is in no way connected to The Giraffe Project, a completely separate organization that has its own training and educational materials.

Giraffe Language

The Giraffe was chosen to symbolize the language of giving and receiving for the following reasons:

- Giraffes have the largest heart of any land animal and this language is meant to connect us with our hearts, i.e., our feelings and needs.
- Giraffes are so tall that they have an unusual advantage; they have a broad perspective and can see many ways to meet needs. Giraffes don't get stuck thinking there is only one way to view a situation. Able to look into the distance, they see the effects of their choices, in the present and in the future.
- Giraffes are willing to "stick their necks out"—to say what is going on inside them and to ask for what they want. This makes them vulnerable to accusations of being self-centered or selfish. But Giraffes also stick their necks out to care about others and hear what is going on in them. This requires the courage to be open, to listen to what others say, and to hear how they respond to what we say.
- A Giraffe perspective, then, includes vision and a big heart—the integration of thinking and feeling.

Many teachers of this language make use of giraffe and jackal puppets and ears to help clarify key distinctions in ways of thinking, talking, and acting. The puppets and ears also provide visual cues for roleplays and contribute fun and laughter to the learning process. (Puppets can be ordered at www.cnvc.org)

We have found that young children and adults alike enjoy the giraffe and jackal symbols for learning this language. However, people between the ages of ten years old and eighteen years old may view them as "childish." As you become more familiar with this language and make it your own, you will find many ways to talk about it, and you can adapt it for the sensibilities of different ages, groups, and cultures.

For simplicity and for fun in this book, we will refer to Giraffe Language in talking about our natural human language of giving and receiving, and we will refer to Jackal Language to talk about our more habitual language of naming and blaming.

Note of caution: When using the giraffe and jackal metaphors, be clear that these are convenient terms that refer to different kinds of thinking, not labels for different kinds of people. We are all capable of not recognizing precious human needs and falling into jackal thinking, listening, and talking. In truth, there are no Jackals or Giraffes, there are only people doing the best they can at each moment to meet their needs.

Giraffe Language helps us:

- Show equal concern for our own needs and the needs of others
- Listen to what's going on in ourselves and others
- Say what we observe

Learning Giraffe is a lot like learning a foreign language: It takes study and practice over time to develop fluency. We may at first feel tongue-tied and awkward; at times, we might doubt that we will ever really learn it. Yet knowing even a little bit of a foreign language increases our ability to communicate. Even early, awkward attempts to use Giraffe Language increase heartfelt connections.

While it is often challenging to change old habits of thinking, listening, and talking, there is plenty of evidence to show that it can be done. Motivation and hope grow as you see how Giraffe Language brings both immediate and long term benefits. Some of these benefits are:

- Clarity about what is important to us
- Deeper connection with ourselves and with others
- Honest communication
- More cooperation, understanding, and respect
- Increased responsibility for ourselves
- Increased sense of "aliveness"
- Increased curiosity

What Game Do You Want to Play?

	☐ The Game of Giving and Receiving	☐ The Game of Naming and Blaming
Goals	To make life wonderful To meet everyone's needs To create community and have power with others	To be right To get what I want To create a hierarchy and have power over others
Motivation	Joy Meeting Needs	Fear, Guilt, Shame, Obligation, Duty
Strategies	**Speak Giraffe Language** Observe: see and hear Share my feelings and needs Make requests **Listen With Empathy** Hear feelings and needs	**Speak Jackal Language** Judge and analyze Blame and criticize Make demands and use punishments and rewards **Listen Without Empathy** Agree or disagree, advise, lecture, scold, argue, sympathize, divert

In the following pages we talk about Intention, Gratitude, and the Four Basic Components of Giraffe Language. This is a concise introduction for readers who are new to Nonviolent Communication, and a helpful reminder or reference for those who are familiar with this communication process. For a more thorough explanation of Giraffe Language, we recommend reading *Nonviolent Communication: A Language of Life* by Marshall B. Rosenberg. To really learn and practice this language, we suggest that you participate in Nonviolent Communication trainings, workshops, and practice groups. (Find information at www.cnvc.org)

When you recognize that all human beings are equal and like yourself in both their desire for happiness and their right to obtain it, you automatically feel empathy and closeness for them . . . True compassion is not just an emotional response but a firm commitment founded on reason.

The Dalai Lama

Intention

Intention is 90 percent of communication. The intention of Giraffe Language is to connect with ourselves and with others, and to engage in a dialogue in order to find a way to meet the needs of all concerned. Our words can be a powerful way to create a connection with others. Without a clear and conscious intention, however, even the most skillfully crafted expression can be hollow.

When the intention is to give and receive from the heart, we try to stay connected to the life that is going on in us from moment to moment. At the same time, we want to stay connected to the feelings and needs of others.

Exercise:

- In your own words, write your intention: What do you want to create in your relationships?

Remembering Your Intention

There are many ways to connect with and nourish intention: taking a moment in the morning to remember it before the day starts, breathing deeply in the middle of an intense interaction and giving ourselves empathy, being in nature, reading inspirational books, meditating, praying, singing, dancing, writing, drawing, painting, etc. Whenever we realign with our intention, our hearts open, and we naturally feel more compassion for ourselves and others.

Exercise:

- What are some ways that you might remember your intention?

Gratitude is the heart's memory.

French Proverb

Gratitude

The more you become a connoisseur of gratitude, the less you are a victim of resentment, depression, and despair. Gratitude will act as an elixir that will gradually dissolve the hard shell of your ego—your need to possess and control—and transform you into a generous being. The sense of gratitude produces true spiritual alchemy, makes us magnanimous—large souled.
— *Sam Keen*

Gratitude is another way to connect with intention. Thinking about the gifts we have given and the gifts we have received provides sustenance for the heart and mind.

Exercise:

- What touches your heart?

- For what are you grateful?

Communication Flow Chart

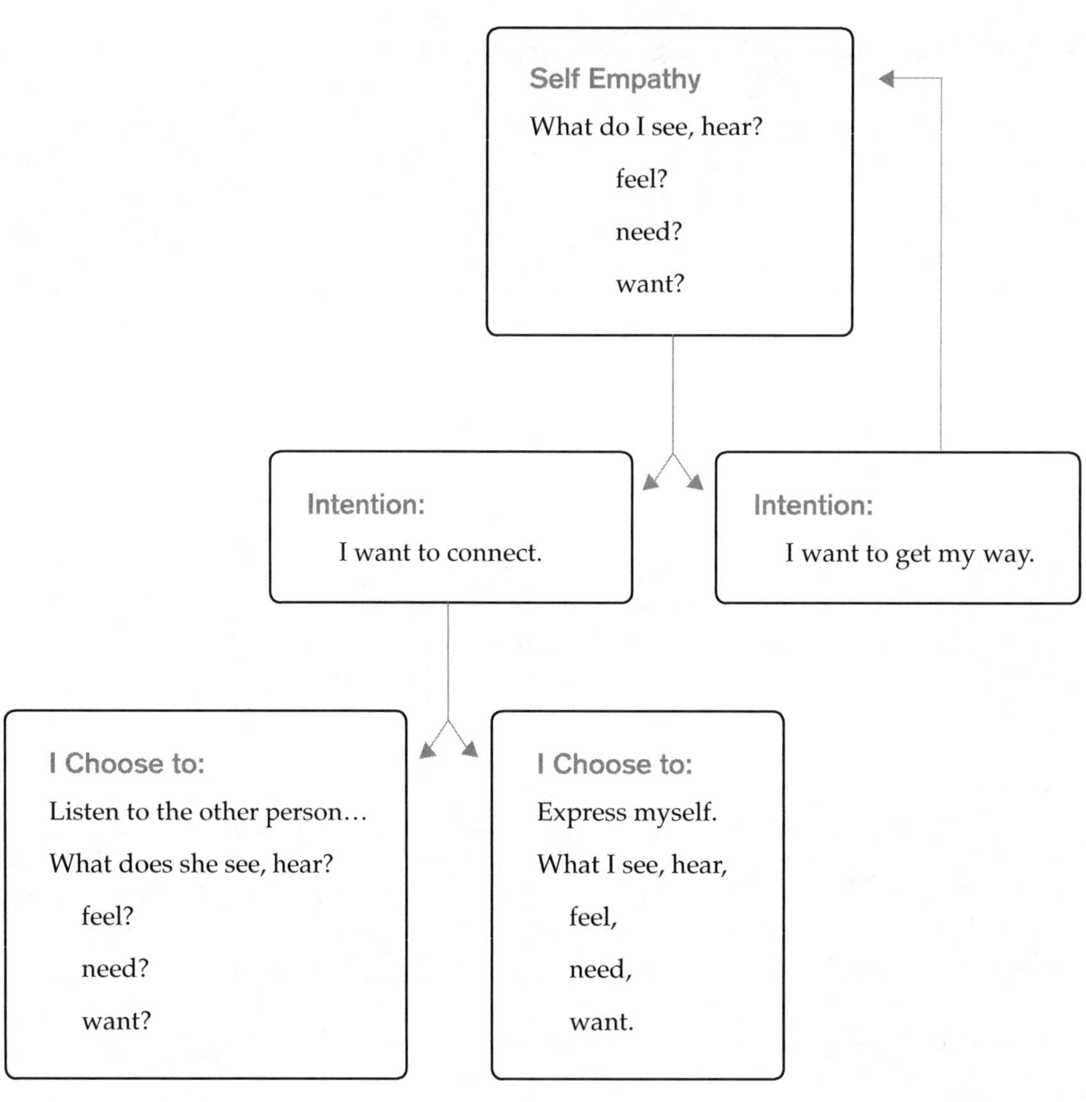

The Flow of Communication

In any interaction there are at least three possible points of connection to life: I can choose to *listen* with empathy to my own feeling and needs, I can *listen* with empathy to the other person's feelings and needs, or I can choose to *express* my feelings and needs.

When interacting with others in Giraffe Language, we engage in a back and forth process of expressing and listening. There are four kinds of information we pay attention to, both when we are expressing and when we are listening: Observations, Feelings, Needs, and Requests (see charts on the next page.) These components of Giraffe Language are developed in a step-by-step fashion in the following pages.

One of the unique features of Giraffe Language is that it only takes one person who knows it to increase understanding and connection in communication.

Marshall Rosenberg

When we focus on Observations, Feelings, Needs, and Requests, we effectively steer clear of criticism, judgment, blame, or demand. Any of these elements of Jackal Language can 1) quickly derail a conversation, 2) take us far away from a heartfelt, meaningful connection with another person, and 3) reduce the chances that everyone's needs will be met.

In any dialogue, there is a kind of traffic flow: sometimes we express and sometimes we listen. It helps to notice the direction of traffic and whose needs are most pressing. When both people in a conversation express at the same time, there is a traffic jam and neither person is heard to his or her satisfaction. Observing the flow of communication, assessing the needs of the moment, and sensing the rhythm of expressing and listening are skills we develop when we learn and practice Giraffe Language.

People often describe a Giraffe dialogue as: "a beautiful dance of connection," "being in the sweet flow of life," and "grace." To do this dance, we *let go of our expectations around the outcome* and trust that in the process strategies will emerge to meet all of our needs; we never know in advance what form those strategies will take.

Giraffe Expressing

I say as honestly as I can: My Observations, Feelings, Needs, and Requests

Observations	I say what I see and hear. *When I hear. . .*
Feelings	I say how I feel. *I feel . . .*
Needs	I say what I need. *because I need . . .*
Requests	I ask for what I predict will meet my needs. *Right now I would like . .* *If you are willing. . .*

Giraffe Listening / Empathy

I make my best guesses about: Your Observations, Feelings, Needs, and Requests

I guess what you see and hear. **Observations**
When you see/ hear. . .

I guess your feelings. **Feelings**
do you feel . . .

I guess your needs. **Needs**
because you need . . . ?

I guess what might help you meet your needs. **Requests**
Right now would you like . . . ?

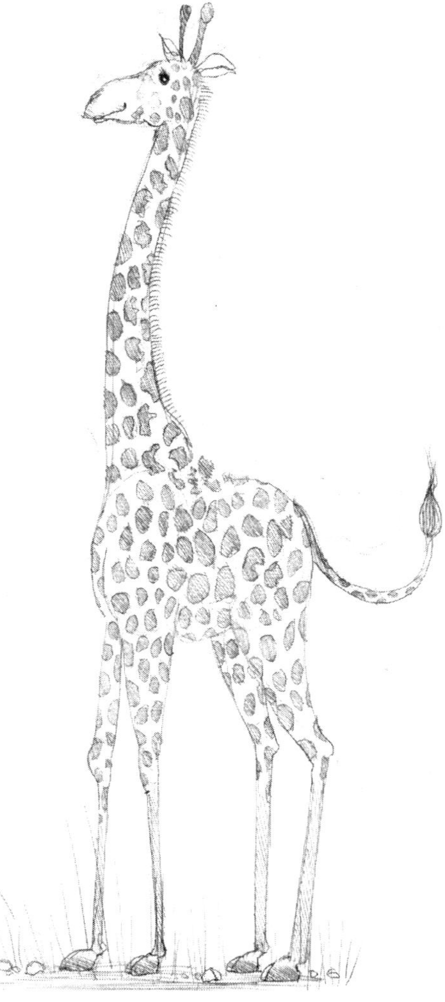

Step One: Observations

> The first component of Nonviolent Communication entails the separation of observation from evaluation. We need to clearly observe what we are seeing, hearing, or touching that is affecting our sense of well-being, without mixing in any evaluation.
>
> *Marshall Rosenberg*

Key Points:

- We clearly describe what we see, hear, feel, remember—without mixing in evaluations.
- We describe something we're reacting to as objectively as if we are looking through the lens of a video camera.
- Evaluations, judgments, or interpretations mixed with our observations are likely to trigger defensiveness in the other person.

Example:

If I say, "You're rude," the other person will likely hear this as a criticism. If, instead, I say: "When I said 'hello' to you this morning, you looked the other way," the other person is likely to agree with my observation and stay open to hearing more.

- When we use observation language, we make our first step of connection with the other person, paving the way for further dialogue.
- When we give observations as feedback to students, we are giving concrete information that can contribute to their learning.

Examples: Imagine how you would feel listening to each of these statements.

Your work is messy. (evaluation)

I see a number of marks in the margins on your paper. (clear observation)

You're a terrible listener. (evaluation)

I see you looking in your book when I'm talking to you. (clear observation)

You're rude. (evaluation)

When I walked up to you today, you ran the other way. (clear observation)

You're irresponsible. (evaluation)

Twice this week you said you'd do your homework, and you didn't turn it in. (clear observation)

When, day after day, teachers use observations separate from evaluations, their students will learn the first step of Giraffe Language—how to make clear observations. (See Chapter 5 for ways students can practice making observations.)

To observe without evaluation is the highest form of human intelligence.

J. Krishnamurti

Step Two: Feelings

Feelings refer to inner experiences or emotions that are connected to needs. When needs are being met, we experience pleasurable feelings such as happy, thrilled, engaged, peaceful. When needs are unmet we experience painful feelings such as upset, sad, fearful, frustrated.

Key Points:

- Feelings can be expressed most simply using just three words. For example, "I feel sad," "I feel worried," "I feel excited," "I feel happy."
- All feelings are okay; in fact, we see them as helpful messengers, telling us about our needs. When we're upset, we know we have important needs that are not being met. When we feel fear, we need safety. When we feel satisfied, we know that our needs are being met.
- We take responsibility for our feelings by expressing them in a way that shows their connection to needs (desires, wants, dreams):

  I feel relieved because I needed understanding, and I got it.

  I feel upset because my need for consideration is not met.

  Are you scared, and would you like assurance you'll be safe?
- When we recognize that feelings are caused by our needs, we are empowered. In contrast, when we think that feelings are caused by the actions of others, we are likely to believe that we are helpless victims.

  Some common expressions in Jackal Language are:

  I'm mad because you . . .

  He makes me happy.

  She makes me irritated.

When teachers use NVC feeling language and distinguish between thoughts and feelings, students will naturally develop a feeling vocabulary and are likely to express feelings more readily. (See Chapter 5 for ways students can practice expressing feelings and listening for feelings.)

Thoughts Disguised as Feelings

While feelings are a vital component of Giraffe Language, they are nearly absent in Jackal Language. Jackal Language is head-talk and steers clear of the concerns and the vulnerability of the heart. Instead, it focuses almost exclusively on thoughts, opinions, and judgments. At times, these are even couched in "feeling language" which contributes to misunderstanding and confusion. An example of this is, "I feel that's unfair." "Unfair" is not a word that describes a feeling; it is a thought that expresses an evaluation. In the following examples of Jackal Language, notice that though the word *feel* is used, we don't know how the speaker is really feeling:

> The heart is the chief feature of a functioning mind.
>
> *Frank Lloyd Wright*

I feel that you're mean.

I feel like I don't matter.

I feel it's not right.

In each of the above statements it would be more accurate to replace the phrase "I feel" with the words "I think."

Even though the following phrases have the word *feel* in them, they are actually going to express thoughts, judgments, or evaluations.

I feel like …

I feel that …

I feel it …

I feel as if …

I feel you/he/she/they …

Faux Feelings

Many words commonly used with the phrase *I feel* are actually evaluations or interpretations of what someone else is doing to us. Some of these false feelings are: abandoned, accepted, attacked, blamed, betrayed, cornered, criticized, dissed, dumped on, ignored, insulted, intimidated, invalidated, left out, let down, manipulated, misunderstood, neglected, patronized, pressured, put down, rejected, ripped off, smothered, threatened, tricked, unheard, unimportant, unseen, and used.

Anger

Anger is a red flag signaling that I have some important needs that are not getting met. Anger is an indication that I am mixing up feelings (usually fear or hurt) with judgmental thoughts. Our thoughts about what others "should" and "shouldn't" do create anger; thoughts about what we (ourselves) "should" do and "shouldn't" do lead to depression.

Hold on to your anger and use it as compost for your garden.

Thich Nhat Hanh

When I'm angry, I can hear three messages:

1) There is something I want very much, and I am not getting it.
2) I am telling myself I *should* have it or someone *should* give it to me.
3) I am about to behave in a way that will guarantee I will not get my needs met.

Expressing Anger in Giraffe

My goal is not to deny, control, or manage my anger. Nor is it to judge myself for feeling angry. Instead, I want to learn from the anger and be able to express it in a way that will best meet my needs. Five things I can do are to:

1) Breathe deeply
2) Take time to notice what's happening in my body
3) Release the other person from responsibility for my feelings
4) Notice the blaming thoughts that are the cause of my anger:
   I'm angry because I'm thinking she should/ he should/ I should…
5) Identify and express the feelings and needs beneath the judgment:
   I feel upset/ hurt/ scared because my need for . . . is not being met.

Feelings List

When Needs Are Met	When Needs Are Not Met
Comfortable, full, satisfied, at ease, relaxed, safe	**Uncomfortable**, uneasy, irritable, unsafe, miserable, embarrassed
Rested, refreshed, energized, alert, relaxed, alive, strong	**Tired**, exhausted, sleepy, dull, weak, foggy, dead
Interested, curious, excited	**Uninterested**, bored, blah
Glad, happy, hopeful, grateful, delighted, jazzed, cheerful	**Sad**, unhappy, disappointed, heavy, lonely, gloomy, bummed
Peaceful, calm, clear, content	**Nervous**, worried, confused, tense
Loving, connected, warm, open, tender, friendly, affectionate	**Mad**, angry, irritated, frustrated, upset, furious, hostile
Grateful, appreciative, thankful	**Annoyed**, disappointed, bitter
Playful, adventurous, alive, inspired, stimulated, eager	**Scared**, afraid, hesitant, shocked, fearful, worried, terrified, stuck

This Feelings List is a resource for expanding and enriching a feeling vocabulary. We suggest that you and your class add to it. For a more extensive list of feeling words, refer to *Nonviolent Communication: A Language of Life* by Marshall Rosenberg or to the Feelings List at www.cnvc.org

Step Three:
Needs

Needs is the word we use in Giraffe Language to describe that which sustains us physically, emotionally, mentally, interpersonally, and spiritually. Needs, and the feelings that arise from them, are moment to moment expressions of how life is moving through us.

Key Points:

- While our cultures, customs, languages, and beliefs differ, we all have the same human needs.
- To stay alive on planet Earth, we need water, air, food, and shelter.
- In addition to survival needs, we have other needs that contribute to our well-being and help us thrive. Some of these needs are: support, love, appreciation, understanding, honesty, autonomy, friendship, learning, and fun.
- When we identify and express our needs, we are more likely to find ways to meet them.
- When we speak of our needs to others, we speak a common human language and create connection, understanding, and compassion.
- When we are as concerned about the needs of others as we are about our own needs, we increase the likelihood that others will want to joyfully give to us.

Distinguishing Between Needs and Strategies

Key Points:

- When we have identified a need we can brainstorm strategies and which one is most likely to satisfy it.
- Needs are never the source of conflict. Conflict arises when we are focused on strategies. We can experience conflict if we are set on one strategy and, in following that action, some other important need of ours does not get met. We can also experience conflict when we are set on one strategy and someone else is set on another strategy that conflicts with ours.
- We can use other words for needs, such as: wants, wishes, values, desires, hopes, dreams, or longings, as long as we distinguish between our needs and the specific strategies we use in our attempts to fulfill them.

Examples:

Need: I value honesty.

Strategy: I ask my student if he would be willing to tell me what he doesn't like about class.

Need: I want consideration for my time.

Strategy: I ask students if they would do their best to be in their seats when the bell rings.

Need: I long for a respectful classroom environment.

Strategy: I ask my students if they would be willing to share with one another and with me what behaviors meet their need for respect.

When teachers talk in terms of needs and separate needs from strategies, students are likely to take more responsibility for meeting their needs. (See Chapter 3 to learn more about needs. See Chapter 5 for activities that help students recognize needs.)

Needs List

We all need:

Fun

Play

Learning

Choices

Physical Nurturance

Air, exercise, food, protection, rest, sexual expression, shelter, touch, water

Relationship With Ourself

Achievement, acknowledgment, authenticity, challenges, clarity, competence, creativity, integrity, knowing our gifts and talents, meaning, privacy, self-development, self-expression, self-worth

Relationship With Others

Appreciation, belonging, to share life's joys and sorrows, closeness, community, consideration, emotional safety, empathy, honesty, interdependence, kindness, love, cooperation, reassurance, respect, sharing gifts and talents, support, to matter to someone, trust, understanding, warmth

Relationship With the World

Beauty, contact with nature, harmony, inspiration, order, peace

This Needs List is not intended to be complete; we encourage you to add to it and refine it.

Step Four: Requests

When we have a strategy in mind for meeting a need, we can ask for help from others to meet the need. By making these requests we provide opportunities for others to give to us. And the requests of others provide us with the opportunity to give to them. In Jackal Language demands are more common than requests and trigger fear, guilt, obligation, or shame rather than a genuine desire to give joyfully.

The objective of Nonviolent Communication is not to change people and their behavior in order to get our way; it is to establish relationships based on honesty and empathy which will eventually fulfill everyone's needs.

Marshall Rosenberg

Key Points

- A request is asking for what we *do* want, not what we *don't* want:

  Please listen carefully to my direction. (What I do want)

  Please don't talk to your neighbors. (What I don't want)

- A request asks for a *present* action:

  Would you be willing to take five minutes now to put your things away? (Present)

  Would you keep your desk neat from now on? (Future)

- A request is stated in *action* language—what we want people "to do" rather than what we want them "to be."

  Would you be willing to lower your voice while I'm reading? (Action)

  Would you be more respectful of others? (Being)

- A request is specific and concrete, not general:

  Would you be willing to work on your math for twenty minutes? (Specific)

  Would you do your work? (General)

- We want others to do as we request only if they are willing to do it.

To make a clear request:

1) Have the intention to make a connection rather than "get your way."

2) Use present, positive, specific, doable action language.

   Would you be willing to tell me what keeps you from getting to class at 9 AM when it starts? (present, positive, doable)

   Will you act responsibly from now on? (vague, no specific action)

3) State the request as a question to show that the other person has a choice about whether or not to do what you ask.

   Would you be willing to work with Jan to make a chart for the science project?

4) Offer empathy if they don't agree to your request. The difference between making a request and making a demand becomes most clear when we hear a "No" in response to our request. If we are upset hearing someone say "No," we have probably made a demand. If we have actually made a request, we can receive their "No" as another possible point of connection.

   A demand:

   Teacher: Would you be willing to help pick up trash during recess?

   Student: No.

   Teacher: You should be willing to help out once in a while.

   A request:

   Teacher: Would you be willing to help pick up trash during recess?

   Student: No.

   Teacher [connecting with the needs behind the "No"]: Is there something that you were looking forward to doing?

When students hear teachers making requests of them rather than demands, they are more likely to make requests also. (See Chapter 5 for activities to help students learn more about requests.)

Examples of Requests:

Connecting Requests

You can make a Connecting Request if you want to create more connection between you and the other person.

Need: I'd like to know whether I'm expressing myself clearly.

Request: Would you be willing to tell me what you heard me say?

Need: I'd like to understand how you are feeling right now.

Request: Would you be willing to tell me?

Need: I'd like to know if you have any reactions to what I said.

Request: Would you be willing to tell me if you do?

Action Requests

You can make an Action Request if you are confident of your connection and want to request or offer a specific action.

Need: I want to focus on the conversation I am having now.

Request: Would you be willing to ask someone else for help?

Need: I want some exercise and I would also like to connect with you.

Request: Would you be willing to go for a walk with me?

Need: I want to contribute to your learning.

Request: Is there something you would like me to do to help with this project?

Giraffe Self-Empathy

I say to *myself* : My Observations, Feelings, Needs, and Requests.

I say what I see and hear.
When I see/ hear . . .

I say what I feel.
I feel . . .

I say what I need.
because I need . . .

I decide what I think
might meet my needs.
Right now I ask myself to . . .

Listening to Myself: Self-Empathy

Practicing Giraffe Language helps to develop the habit of frequently checking in with what is going on in ourselves—noticing our own feelings and needs. When we do this, we meet needs for connection with ourselves and compassion for ourselves.

Key Points

- When I am not connected to my own feelings and needs, I am not able to connect with others. In fact, when I find myself unable to empathize with others, that is a clear signal that *I need empathy.*
- When I feel pleasurable feelings—happy, excited, joyful, satisfied—self-empathy is a way to privately acknowledge and celebrate the needs that *have been met.* Whenever I acknowledge that my needs have been met, I build confidence in my ability to meet needs in the future.
- When I feel painful feelings—upset, hurt, worried, angry—taking the time to connect with my feelings and needs most often provides comfort, understanding, and compassion for myself. When I feel confused, listening to my thoughts and inner dialogue can create clarity.

  Self-Empathy can be especially helpful when I'm talking nonstop, I'm defensive, I'm arguing, I'm angry, I'm depressed, or I can't hear the feelings and needs of others.

  Most often, Self-Empathy focuses on what I observe, what I feel, and what I need.

The insight into our inner world allows us to connect to everything around us, so that we can see quite clearly the oneness of all that lives.

Sharon Salzburg

Examples:

When I heard myself use such a loud voice with the students today, I felt sad because I didn't create the connection with them that I wanted.

Having completed that chapter of the book, I feel pleased because I want to complete this project for class tomorrow.

I feel confused and want more clarity.

Listening to Others: Empathy

Empathy is a respectful understanding of what others are experiencing. Instead of offering empathy, we often have a strong urge to give advice or reassurance and to explain our own position or feeling. Empathy, however, calls upon us to empty our mind and listen to others with our whole being.

—Marshall Rosenberg

Empathy is the intention to connect with the feelings and needs of another. It is giving the gift of our presence—without judgment, analysis, suggestions, stories, or any motivation to fix the other person.

Key Points

- When we empathize with another person, we listen for their feelings and needs even, and especially, when their words sound like criticism, blame, or judgment.
- Giving empathy can meet mutual needs for connection, understanding, and compassion.
- Giving empathy does not mean that we necessarily agree with the other person or that we will do what was requested.
- Empathy is not dependent on words and is often silent. However, if it seems helpful to express empathy verbally, NVC suggests that we guess the other person's feelings and needs. This shows a respectful understanding for the fact that we never know for sure what another person feels and needs. Whether you are accurate or not, guessing what another person *might* be feeling and needing has a powerful effect. Your guesses help her focus on how she actually is and clarify what would make life more wonderful for her.

When we express empathy verbally, we use the four steps of NVC as a guideline—Observations, Feelings, Needs, and Requests—this time, in the form of a question:

Observation: When you think about the time you've spent on this problem,

Feeling: are you feeling discouraged

Need: because you wanted to see a solution by now?

Request: Would you like to hear some ideas I have?

In most empathic responses we guess just feelings and needs. The observation is often understood, and by talking in Giraffe Language with the person we are meeting the implied request for empathy.

Feeling: Are you frustrated,

Need: And wish this was easier?

Listening is an attitude of the heart, a genuine desire to be with another which both attracts and heals.

J. Isham

Instead of expressing empathy, we often express non-empathically:

Advising: I think you should . . .

Commiserating: That's terrible. She had no right to do that to you.

Consoling: Everything's going to be okay.

Correcting: It's not really that hard.

Educating: You can learn from this.

Explaining: I didn't want to do it this way, but . . .

Evaluating: If you hadn't been so careless . . .

Fixing: What will help you is to . . .

Interrogating: What are you feeling? When did you start feeling this way?

One-upping: You should hear what happened to me . . .

Shutting down: Don't worry. It's not so bad.

Story-telling: That reminds me of the time . . .

Sympathizing: You poor thing.

Translating Jackal to Giraffe

Jackal Language	Giraffe Language	Why Translate?
I can't . . .	*I don't want to, I won't* *I choose not to* *I haven't learned how to*	To acknowledge choice
I feel that . . .	*I think, I believe* *I have an opinion* *It seems to me*	To distinguish between thoughts and feelings
Why? What? And probing questions	*Are you feeling?* *Are you wishing?* *I'd like to know . . .*	To connect with what's alive right now
It's right, wrong, good, bad, smart, stupid.	*I judge it to be* *I believe it is*	To acknowledge subjectivity of my perception and judgment
It (you, he, she) makes me sick. *It makes me happy.*	*I feel sick.* *I feel happy.*	To own my feelings
All, always, never	Give specific situations: *When . . .*	To acknowledge limitations of my knowledge and avoid judgment of a situation

What Language Are You Using?

☐ Giraffe Language	☐ Jackal Language
Acknowledges Choice I choose to, I want to, I can. There are many ways to meet needs.	**Denies Choice** I have to, I must. I can't. There's only one way.
Perceives Abundance There's enough if we share. Everyone's needs can be met. It's you and me.	**Perceives Scarcity** There's not enough to go around. We can't meet everyone's needs. It's you or me.
Observes and Expresses I see, I hear, I remember . . .	**Evaluates and Judges** Here's what happened . . . You're too . . . He's mean; she's rude.
Takes Responsibility for My Own Feelings and Needs I feel . . . *because I need* . . .	**Blames Others/ Blames Self** I feel . . . *because you* . . .
Asks for What I Would Like Here's what I'd like. If you're willing.	**Makes Demands** You have to . . . If you don't . . .
Listens Empathically Are you feeling . . .? because you need . . .?	**Listens Selectively** Suggests, lectures, advises, argues, fixes, analyzes

What Language Do You Want To Use?

Putting It All Together

Teacher-Student Dialogues

The following teacher-student dialogues are examples of the giraffe dance of honesty and empathy in the classroom. These dialogues are distillations of real classroom situations; they necessarily sound more stilted than the real-life dialogues where body language, facial expression, tone of voice, silence, and humor add color, tone, and meaning to communication. Nevertheless, we hope that in reading these dialogues, you will get some feel for how the conscious intent to connect, coupled with some facility with Nonviolent Communication, creates a flow of connection between people, even when only one person knows NVC.

When teachers first hear about NVC, they often say that they don't have time for this kind of dialogue. Our experience is that taking the time to listen empathically to students and show that we care about their needs decreases behavioral problems that require a teacher's attention. At the same time, there is more engaged learning and more efficient use of time for both students and teachers.

What's Worth Learning?

A sixth grade teacher is trying to explain a math concept to her class. There are three students communicating with each other primarily through eye contact, comments, and outbursts of laughter. Twice, the teacher asks the students if they would please listen to what she is saying. Each time, after initially giving her their attention, they go back to talking with one another. Distracted from what she is trying to teach and increasingly frustrated with her attempts to get their attention, the teacher notices that she is getting angry and is judging the students as "rude" and "obnoxious," which she knows will just add to her anger and decrease her ability to connect with them. Remembering that underneath anger are important needs not being met, she turns her attention inside herself for a moment to connect with her needs.

> **Teacher**, silently "venting" her anger to herself: *This is ridiculous. I've had it with these kids! All they want to do is goof off!* . . . Then, silent self-empathy—connecting with the feelings and needs beneath the anger: *So what am I feeling? I'm so frustrated trying to get their attention. I'm angry because I'm telling myself that they're "goofing off" and being disrespectful... Underneath the anger, I see that I'm frustrated and sad because I really want to get this concept across to everyone at the same time; I really want to connect with them, not fight with them.*

Now in touch with her feelings, needs, and desire to connect with these students, she turns to them and expresses her observations, feelings and needs, then makes a request:

> **Teacher** [expressing]: Hearing you continue to talk to each other after asking you twice to please listen while I'm explaining this math concept, I feel frustrated and sad. I want to finish this explanation and move on, and I need cooperation to do that. I'd like to know if you'd be willing to be quiet and listen to me for the next ten minutes so I can finish talking and then find out what you've learned?

Student 1: This is so boring!

Teacher [shifting to empathic listening—guessing the student's feelings and needs]:

Are you antsy and wish we were doing something more active?

Student 1: Yes, I hate doing nothing but listening.

Teacher: Do you want me to hear how hard it is for you to just sit and listen when you want to be active and participating more?

Student 1: Yes.

Teacher [noticing that Student 1 has relaxed somewhat after she realized she had been heard, she expresses]:

I'm puzzled and disappointed right now because I'd like to have a more interactive, fun way to get this concept across, and I haven't thought of one yet. I recognize that we all have different learning preferences. Some of us can sit and listen for quite a long time while others really want to be active and work with materials or talk with others. Would someone be willing to tell me what you heard me say so I know whether or not I am making myself clear?

Student 4: You said we each learn differently and you want us to be able to learn the way that works best.

Teacher: Thank you. Yes, I feel happiest when everyone's engaged in learning. And I want to make lessons as lively as possible.

Teacher [turning to the other two students]: Are you also impatient with listening right now?

Student 2: Yeah. And I don't even understand why we have to learn this stuff?

Student 3: Yeah, we'll never use it.

Teacher [empathizing—guessing the students' feelings and needs beneath their words]:

Sounds like you're also feeling frustrated because you'd like to know what value there could be for you to learn this?

Student 2: Yeah. Why waste time learning something you'll never use?

Teacher [empathizing—hearing more needs]: Would you like to know that what you're spending your time and energy on will be useful to you some time in the future?

Student 2: Yeah.

Teacher [sensing a shift in all three students after being heard this way, and noticing that they are now giving their full attention to her, she expresses what's going on for her]: I'm really glad you told me this. I see I haven't made clear to you the value I see in your learning this concept. I'd really like to do that because I don't want you spending your time and energy on something you don't see as useful. I would like to continue with this important discussion of what's valuable to you and come back to the math later. Would you be willing to join me?

[Seeing heads nod, she turns to the rest of the class to find out what their understanding is]: So, I'd like to know if anyone else is unclear about the value of learning this math? Will you raise your hands if you're unclear? [She looks around . . .] So, about half of you are unclear. How about the other half? Would anyone who *does* see value in learning this be willing to share with the rest of the class the value you see? After hearing from those who want to speak, I'd like to tell you why I see value in teaching this to you.

In the conversation that ensues, the teacher and the students discuss what value they can see in learning the math that the teacher was trying to teach. Together they brainstorm a few different ways that they could learn the concept.

In the dialogue, the teacher communicates at least four important messages to her students: I care about your feelings and needs, I recognize and value the diverse learning styles and preferences in the class, I want you to see value in what you are studying and learning, and I am willing to take the time to explore the value there could be in studying this concept.

"Bully"

Coming in from recess, a teacher heard one of her third grade students, Erin, yell to another student, "You're a bully."

In the past, she might have just reminded the student that we don't call people names and then send the accused bully to the office. But this time she knew that her automatic reaction wouldn't get to the root of the problem. In fact, she was pretty sure that it would only increase tension between these two students. She asked Erin if she would talk with her for a few minutes.

Teacher [expressing her feelings and needs]: I feel sad hearing you say, "You're a bully" to Bob, because I want us to learn how to talk to one another without using put-downs. Would you be willing to tell me what you're hearing me say?

Student: You're saying I shouldn't talk like that.

Teacher: Thank you for telling me what you heard. I'd like you to hear something different. What I'd like you to hear is that I'm sad because respect for all people is important to me, and calling people names doesn't show the respect I'd like to see. Would you be willing to tell me what you're hearing me say now?

Student: You don't want us to call people names because it doesn't show respect.

Teacher: Yes, that's just what I wanted to communicate. I'd like for us to tell each other how we feel, what's bothering us, and what we want in a way that's honest and respectful. Is this something you'd like as well?

Student: Bob is really mean.

Teacher [listening for Erin's feelings and needs]: Are you feeling angry and upset because you'd like to be treated with kindness?

Student: Yeah, he's always mean to me.

Teacher: I'd like to understand what you're calling "mean." Would you be willing to tell me something Bob did that seemed "mean" to you?

Student: He told me I couldn't play ball with the other kids. He said I was too small and "stupid" to play.

Teacher [empathizing—guessing Erin's feelings and needs]: I imagine you had a lot of different feelings going on at the same time. I'm guessing you were disappointed because you wanted to play?

Student: Yeah. I never get to play.

Teacher [trying to obtain more clarity]: So there are other times besides today that this happens?

Student: Lots of times. It's always Bob that won't let me.

Teacher: Hmmmm . . . . I'm guessing you're pretty upset and maybe even discouraged, wondering if you'll ever be allowed to play in that game?

Student [bursting into tears]: Yeah . . . I want to have fun, too . . . I'm a good player.

Teacher: So are you puzzled and wonder why you aren't getting a chance to play?

Student: Yeah, I want to know why he doesn't like me. And I want him to stop calling me names.

Teacher: I'm hearing that you are sad and upset, too, because you'd like people to be honest with you and tell you what's really going on, without calling you names?

Student [suddenly standing up straight]: Yes. I want him to talk to me.

Teacher: I wonder if you would be willing to meet with Bob and tell him how you feel about the situation, and what you'd like?

Student: If you'll be there too.

Teacher: You'd feel more comfortable if I'm there?

Student: Yeah.

Teacher: I'd be willing to do that.

In this dialogue Erin received enough empathy from the teacher to get in touch with her feelings and needs, which later made it possible for her to express them to Bob. The teacher helped Bob to reflect back what he heard Erin say. The teacher also expressed how important it was to her that they treat one another with respect and that they use words to say what's going on with them. Bob seemed to take this in, although, he was mostly silent and obviously in a lot of pain.

In a subsequent conversation between Bob and the teacher, Bob expressed feelings of hurt and anger stemming from the changes in his household since his new baby sister was born. Bob discovered that he could find understanding and relief from painful feelings by talking about them rather than by acting aggressively toward other students.

The Gift of "No"

Marianne Gothlin, a teacher at the Skarpnack's Free School in Stockholm, Sweden, tells the following story:

At our school, parents, teachers, and students take responsibility for the care and maintenance of the school buildings and grounds. The students form groups to care for different areas of the school. Over the years, I have experienced such joy seeing how much fun the students have cooperating to take care of daily life in school.

Shortly after the school opened the students agreed that they would all participate in setting the tables for lunch. This activity seemed particularly fun for them, so I was somewhat surprised when a new student—an eight-year-old boy—exclaimed one day, "I am not going to set tables no matter what you say!"

I know that at many schools, his strong expression of resistance would be considered unacceptable. He might be told something like, "Everyone has to do work here, and you're no exception." He might be quickly labeled as "difficult" or "spoiled." I understand why these judgments come so easily to mind.

Now that I practice NVC, when students say "No" to a request I have made, I become very curious and interested. I've learned to recognize that behind every "No" is something important that they're saying "Yes" to. I really want to know what is so important to them. In this case, I sensed that this was not a matter of a momentary desire to do something other than set tables but something far more important.

Teacher: I would really like to understand what's going on for you. When you're asked to help set the tables do you feel upset because you were not part of the group when they chose to do this?

Student: No!

Teacher: [continuing to guess his feelings and needs]: Do you feel angry because you would like to have freedom to choose whether you will set tables right now?

Student [raising his voice to a scream]: No! And I am not going to set any tables no matter what you say, and I don't want to listen to you!

The student then ran away and hid himself in another room. I followed him, sat down next to him and kept quiet for a few minutes. Then he started to weep. My intuition told me to ask him about his experience setting tables at lunch when he went to another school.

Teacher: Would you be willing to tell me something to help me understand what keeps you from wanting to set tables?

The student continued to weep.

Teacher: I wonder whether your experience setting tables at your other school makes it really hard to enjoy setting tables here?

Student [crawling into my arms and crying]: At my last school, setting tables was a punishment, and I was one of the boys who had to do it the most because I was always late coming in from the breaks.

Teacher: Oh . . . no wonder this doesn't seem like a fun thing to do. I'm really grateful that you are telling me this. And I feel sad hearing that the teachers didn't find a different way to get you to class on time.

Student: I set the table almost every day last year.

Teacher [feeling touched and sad to hear this]: I really understand how you would not enjoy the thought of setting tables now. . . I would like us to find a solution together . . . Would you be willing to bring this up with the rest of the group? We can see if they are willing to support you in waiting to set tables until it would be fun for you.

Student: I don't think they would agree to such a suggestion.

Teacher: I'm confident that the other students would understand if you tell them what you told me. I'll be there to help you. Would you be willing to do that?

Student: Maybe.

At first, this student was surprised and hesitant, hearing my suggestion; then, he agreed to talk to the students with my help.

He told his story to the class and asked the students to raise their hands if they could agree to let him wait to set tables until he could do it happily. When he saw all but two of the students raising their hands—one of them being his little sister—he felt overwhelmed with joy and relief. The next morning in the classroom he raised his hand and asked to share something. He said with a big smile, "I just want you all to know that yesterday, when you raised your hands, I felt so happy." This happened on a Tuesday and on Friday he came up and asked if he could set tables with the group.

The Power of Thirty Minutes

The principal of a Cleveland area elementary school attended a one-day introductory NVC workshop and knew immediately that she wanted her whole school to learn these skills. She arranged for three days of intensive training for the entire staff of her building.

When a second grade teacher returned to her classroom after the training, the children seemed restless and unsettled. She stopped the lesson and called them together.

> **Teacher**: You don't seem to be able to settle down today. What's going on?
>
> **Student 1**: I don't know. It's not fun to be in school anymore.
>
> **Teacher:** Is something different?
>
> **Student 2:** The substitute teacher was mean, and she didn't even know our names!
>
> **Teacher:** So you didn't like having a substitute for the last three days?
>
> **Student 3:** No! She changed everything around!
>
> **Teacher:** Do you feel upset, and want me to hear that you missed all our regular routines?
>
> **Student 3:** Yeah! Why did you go away and leave us? You were gone for so long!

Teacher: So you missed me, too, and want to know where I have been for the last three days?

Everyone: Yeah!!

Teacher: I went to a class to learn how we can all talk to each other so nobody ends up being bad or getting into trouble. Would you like me to teach you how to do that?

With the children's assent, the teacher spent the next thirty minutes teaching the class the NVC skills she had spent three days learning.

One boy in the classroom was known to get upset very quickly whenever another child came near or started to talk to him while he was trying to work. His usual response was to yell, push, and shove, which often escalated into a disruptive scene. This happened at least once or twice a day.

Soon after the students' thirty-minute NVC introduction, a child came up to this boy and started talking to him. For the first time, instead of the usual lashing out, he behaved in a very different manner. He stomped over to the computer and typed out this message, which he then proceeded to read out loud: "When you come close and talk to me when I am trying to work, I feel frustrated because I want my privacy and my space. Would you please leave me alone until I say OK?"

From then on, the other children in the class were more aware of respecting this boy's need for space, and if any of them forgot, he knew how to remind them!

Chapter 5
Develop Skills Through Activities and Games

In this chapter you will find a collection of activities and games that NVC trainers and classroom teachers have created and used with young people to teach and practice Nonviolent Communication skills.

We offer the following suggestions for fun and learning:

- Offer these activities to your students with an invitation to play. We predict that the fun factor will be high as long as children do not hear a demand to play.
- Most of these activities can be used as is or adapted for play with all ages. We imagine that you and your students will enjoy some of them more than others. If you don't see a way to use a particular activity with your students, read the objective for that activity and see what ideas come up for you as fun ways to teach and practice that objective. We hope they will inspire you and your students to create your own ways to practice NVC skills.

To meet our need to contribute to more learning and fun for teachers and students:

We welcome additional activities for future printings of this book. We invite you to send us activities or games you have created and/or used in your classroom to teach and practice NVC skills. We will acknowledge receipt of these gifts and consider them for inclusion in future printings of *The Compassionate Classroom*.

Contributors to this section of activities and games include:

Diane Arrigoni, Marcelline Brogli, Marilyn Fiedler, Jillian Froebe, Pamela Fuller, Sura Hart, Rita Herzog, Patty Hodgson, Lois Hudson, Holley Humphrey, Inbal Kashtan, Miki Kashtan, Elizabeth Kerwin, Victoria Kindle Hodson, Marlene Maskornick, Liv Monroe, Natasha Rice, Robin Rose, and Fred Sly.

Some Reflection Questions for the Activities

- Is there something you liked about this activity?
- Is there something you didn't like?
- What feelings came up for you during this activity?
- What needs were met for you? Any needs not met?
- Did this activity help you learn something about yourself? About the group? About the world?
- Can you think of ways that what you learned could help you in your life?

Skill-building Activities and Games

Topic: Observations

Title:	Listen! Listen! Listen!
Objective:	To increase listening skills
Type of activity:	Interactive activity using sound
Group size:	Entire class
Space/time:	Classroom/10+ minutes
Materials	Rhythm and sound instruments, jars filled with beans, or recorded sounds

Procedures for several activities:

- Display rhythm instruments or other musical instruments. Ask students to close their eyes while one person plays or sounds each one. Students try to guess which instrument is being sounded. If they do not guess accurately, help them by giving clues (e.g. *It's a bigger instrument. It's a string instrument.)* without using the words/concepts *right* and *wrong*.

  * Make clapping or snapping patterns with your hands or fingers. Asking students to repeat each pattern. Students can take turns making up their own patterns for others to repeat.

  * Sound bottles: use identical jars with lids and varying amounts of beans in each. Blindfold students and ask them to put the jars in order from those that sound the softest/highest to those that sound the loudest/lowest.

  * Play a tape of familiar and not-so-familiar sounds, stopping for the children to guess each one. Express appreciation for a wide variety of guesses, rather than looking for the "right" answer.

  * Visit a particular place in school, a corner of the playground, etc. Have children close their eyes and listen. When they return to class, ask them to describe what they heard.

  * Students can write poems about sounds they hear: *Summer Sounds, Fall Sounds, Classroom Sounds, Kitchen Sounds*

Topic: Observations

Title:	Is That an Observation?
Objective:	To distinguish between observations and evaluations
Type of activity:	Writing, sorting, discussing, game playing
Group size:	Up to 30, working in pairs and whole group
Space/time:	Tables for pairs to work/30 minutes
Materials:	1 envelope holding about 50 statement strips, clear tape or glue, 1 piece of grey construction paper (6"x18"), 1 piece of colored construction paper (6"x18"), 1 piece of white construction paper (6"x18")

Procedure:

1. Review the difference between observations and evaluations.
2. Form pairs and ask each pair to write headings on the construction paper: OBSERVATION on the grey paper, EVALUATION on the colored paper, and "?" on the white paper (for statements they are uncertain about).
3. Partners read each statement strip and discuss whether it's an observation or an evaluation and then tape or glue the strips onto the designated paper.
4. When all pairs are finished, meet in the large group to share what was learned and to discuss any statements that were put in the "not sure" category.

Variation: Concentration Game

Laminate a set of strips to use to play Concentration. Place all the strips face down. The first player turns over any two strips. If the statements form a pair (two observations or two evaluations), the player keeps them and turns over two more. If the strips do not form a pair, they are turned over, face down, and the next player takes a turn.

Is That an Observation? — Statement Strips

She gave me a cookie.	She is generous.
I ended up bleeding the last time we played together.	You play too rough.
He asked me to join the game.	He is really friendly.
They are pressing their noses against the window.	They're acting stupid.
She burped.	That's rude.
You finished ten math problems.	You worked so hard.
You are sitting with your legs stretched out.	You are taking up too much room.
She put mustard on her apple.	That's gross.
He read two books this week.	He's smart.
You sat on my glasses. Now they are cracked.	You stupid idiot.
You bumped into me.	You are so clumsy.
He pushed me out of line.	He's a bully.
You stayed inside after I asked you to come out.	You are a poor sport.
You ate the last two pieces of pie.	You are a selfish pig.
She said I couldn't join the game.	That's mean.

Is That an Observation? — Statement Strips

He told the teacher that I took his pencil.	He's a tattletale.
She came to see me when I was sick.	She is a good friend.
I spent two hours doing homework.	You play too rough.
There's glue on the table and on the floor.	We have too much homework.
She told me I had to use blue paint, not green.	Our teacher is cruel.
He kept asking me questions when I was trying to write.	You always make a mess.
I saw you kick the ball onto the roof, and then I heard you tell the teacher that you didn't do it.	She's too bossy.
	He's always bugging me.
He said he wouldn't climb the tree.	You are a liar.
I hear you talking when I am trying to read.	What a wimp! He's a big baby.
I saw you pick up my pencil and put it on your desk.	You are so annoying.
They said no one else could be in their club.	You're always distracting me.
She walked away when we said we didn't want to play kickball.	You stole my pencil again, you thief.
You didn't move out of my way when I asked you to.	They think they're so cool.
She kicked my chair.	She always wants things her way.

Topic: Observations

Title:	Nature Walk
Objective:	To increase skills in observation
Type of Activity:	Walking in nature, writing and/or art
Group Size:	Entire Class
Space/Time:	Outdoors and place to draw or write/30+ minutes
Materials:	Paper plates, glue, a small bag for each child

Procedure:

Version 1

1. Go on a nature walk. Each child collects objects on the ground: leaves, twigs, pine cones, small pebbles, seed pods, etc.
2. When they return, children choose one object, observe it carefully, and then describe it verbally or in writing. (Do this orally for younger students; older students or adults can write.)
3. Children can glue one or more objects on a paper plate and attach the written description below the object.

Version 2

1. Students go for a nature walk in pairs.
2. One child closes his/her eyes and listens while the partner describes a particular tree, shrub, plant, cloud, etc. that is visible.
3. Then the student opens his eyes and tries to identify what it was that his partner described.

Variations and Extensions:

Children choose one object, make a sketch or painting of the object, and use the object as a stimulus to write a story.

Topic: Observation

Title:	Detective Pairs
Objective:	To distinguish between observations and evaluations
Type of Activity:	Interactive game
Group Size:	6–20
Space/Time:	Classroom/30–60 minutes
Materials:	Make 20 flashcards: 10 with an evaluation on them (marked "E") and 10 with the corresponding observations (marked "O").

Procedure:

1. Create a deck of cards by selecting the number of matching pairs needed for each student to have one card.
2. Shuffle cards and give one to each student.
3. One student with an "E" evaluation card reads it aloud.
4. The student who has the "O" observation card that corresponds to the evaluation just read, reads her card aloud.
5. The students with matching cards form pairs after everyone has read their card.

Variations and Extensions:

- Everyone picks a card and either goes to one corner of the room marked "Observations" or to another corner marked "Evaluations." They then proceed to find their partners.
- Everyone picks a card and the group mingles until each student finds his/her partner.
- Once the dyads are formed, they create a new observation and evaluation and make new cards for future games.
- Words to be used with younger children could be "fact" and "opinion" rather than "observation" and "evaluation."
- This activity can be used to form dyads for other activities.

Detective Flash Cards

Your paper's messy.	There are holes and smudges on your paper.	That's a dumb idea.	I have another idea.
They're acting silly.	They are rolling around on the floor.	She's nosy.	She asked me questions about what I did yesterday.
He's a good student.	He finishes his work before other students.	They are mean.	They said I couldn't have a turn.
She threw a fit.	She beat her fist on the chair.	He doesn't care about other people.	He often cuts in front of others in line.
I read a long book.	I read a book with 173 pages.	She's greedy.	She took the last three pieces of pizza.
He's a tattletale.	He told the teacher that I called him a name.	He is a genius.	He figured out a math problem before I did.
You are so hyper.	You are moving back and forth in your chair, and the chair is tipping.	She's a dictator.	She said I had to turn the jumprope.
She's nice.	She gave me an invitation to her birthday party.	They think they're so great.	They said that I couldn't sit at their table.

Detective Flash Cards

That's yucky.	He put pickles in his soup.	What a brat!	He took the ball and threw it in the street.
It was a horrible movie.	I did not enjoy this movie.	You are the teacher's pet.	The teacher asked you to pass out the treats.
He is so rude.	He took my skateboard without asking.		
Beulah is mean.	Beulah called me stupid.		
She is a tattletale.	She told other people what I told her.		
He's just trying to get attention.	He wore his football uniform to school.		
She's always showing off.	She combed her hair during class.		
He's always showing off.	He dyed his hair purple and green.		

Topic: Observations

Title:	Fortune Cookies
Objective:	To distinguish between observations and evaluations
Type of Activity:	Game
Group Size:	5–15
Space/Time:	Classroom/20 minutes
Materials:	Fortune cookies: tan paper squares or circles 3–4" across (5–10 per student), three-column chart with headings: Fortune, Observation, Evaluation

Procedure:

1. Give one fortune cookie to each student. One at a time, have each student open his cookie and read the fortune. Ask if it is really a fortune or if it is an observation or an evaluation. Record in the appropriate column on the flip chart while they munch on their cookies.
2. When all students have read their "fortunes," each writes her own "fortune" (fortune, observation, or evaluation.) This can be done on 3–4" round or square pieces of tan paper that are then folded twice to resemble fortune cookies. You can ask older students to write one statement for each category on the chart.
3. "Cookies" are put into a bowl. One at a time, each student selects a cookie, reads it and says whether it is a fortune, observation, or evaluation. After feedback from the group, student tapes the paper in the appropriate column on the flip chart.

Variations and Extensions:

You can order custom fortune cookies from:
Custom Fortune Cookie Company
6204 Evergreen • Houston, Texas 77081 • (713) 998-2524
info@customfortunecookie.com

Topic: Feelings

Title:	Books of Feelings
Objectives:	To recognize that everyone has feelings and that we may experience different feelings in response to the same events
Type of Activity:	Writing and drawing
Group Size:	Any
Space/Time:	Tables or other space for drawing/20+ minutes
Materials:	Paper for the book pages, pencils, pens, or paints, materials for book covers (construction paper, manila folders, gift paper, wallpaper)

Procedure:

1. In large or small groups, ask students to think of times when they feel scared. To stimulate discussion you can read a story or show illustrations that are likely to elicit feelings.
2. Ask each child to draw a picture illustrating his own situation.
3. Compile into a class book titled "I Feel Scared When . . ."

Variations and Extensions:

1. Create additional books: "I Feel Peaceful when ______," "I Feel Frustrated when______," and "I Feel Curious when ______."
2. In the large group, ask students to decide what feeling and what situation they would like to illustrate. Compile all the illustrated situations into a class book titled something like "We All Have Feelings."

Topic: Feelings & Needs

Title:	Feeling Leaves
Objective:	To see the connection between feelings and needs: Feelings arise from our met and unmet needs
Type of Activity:	Art
Group Size:	5–30
Space/Time:	Classroom/30 minutes
Materials:	Green squares of paper for leaves, a large poster with two large trees, each with many bare branches. One tree has upturned branches and is labeled When Needs Are Met, and the other tree has downturned branches labeled When Needs Are Unmet

Procedure:

1. Introduce the concept of universal needs and create a Needs List prior to this activity. (See Needs List in Chapter 4.)
2. Ask, "Where do feelings come from?" and listen to students' answers.
3. Suggest that all of our feelings come from our needs. Some feelings arise when our needs are met. ("What feelings do you have when your need for hunger is met? For play? For learning something new?") Other feelings arise when our needs are not met. ("What feelings do you have when your need for rest is not met? For respect? For friends?")
4. Each student folds a piece of green paper in half, then tears it around the edges to make a leaf. Ask them to write a feeling word on the leaf. (You could have pre-cut leaves with feeling words written on them.) Students then take turns placing leaves on the corresponding tree. (Note: Some feeling words, like "surprise" could go on either tree.)

Topic: Feelings

Title:	Triangle E/motions
Objective:	To understand that people have different feeling reactions to the same situation
Type of Activity:	Movement
Group Size:	Any
Space/Time:	Space to move around/20+ minutes
Materials:	Three large signs, each marked with either Anger, Fear, Hurt

Procedure:

1. The three signs are placed in an approximate triangle around the room, with one word on each: Anger, Fear (scared), Hurt (sad).
2. Read a statement and direct the students to move to wherever they want to go in the triangle that most closely represents how they might feel in response to that situation. If they imagine they would feel primarily one of the three feelings, they would go to the corresponding corner. If they have a mix of feelings, they would go to a spot that represents that mix. If nothing inside the triangle fits for them, they can step outside the triangle.
3. Read statements, one at a time, until interest wanes. Discuss:

   What did you notice about this game?

   What feelings did you have watching people move to different corners of the room?

   How did you feel letting people know how you feel in these situations?

   What did you learn?

Statements (adapt to suit your class):

1. One of your classmates calls you "stupid" in class.
2. You see a bigger child push a smaller child.
3. You hear someone make a joke about someone in your class.
4. You make a lot of mistakes on your math assignment.
5. Someone you want to play with says she doesn't want to play with you.
6. You fall down and rip your new shirt.
7. Your best friend tells you he doesn't want to be your friend anymore.
8. You're late to school for the second day in a row.
9. Your friend said she would call you after school, and she doesn't.
10. It's a half hour after your mom said she'd pick you up, and she still hasn't come.

Adapted from the *CNVC Module Training,* © 2002 Inbal Kashtan and Miki Kashtan and the Center for Nonviolent Communication.

Topic: Feelings

Title:	Three Little Words
Objective:	To translate disowned feelings (blame) into owned feelings
Type of Activity:	Demonstration, discussion
Group Size:	Entire class
Space/Time:	A circle so everyone can see each other/ 15+ minutes
Materials:	Solid rubber ball, wooden block, eraser, peanuts, pomegranate

Procedure:

Discuss the concept of "owned" and "disowned" feelings. We "own" our feelings when we recognize them and take responsibility for them. We "disown" feelings when we make other people responsible for them.

If students can see and/or feel the energy drain of disowned feelings and choose to speak with ownership, it can open up a whole new world of clarity, honesty, and responsibility. As soon as we say someone else "made me feel," we have given away our power. We reclaim our power when we own our feelings using three little words: *"I feel ______."*

Demonstration:

Teacher demonstrates by holding up a solid rubber ball:

"Sometimes things are hidden from plain sight. Do you think there's anything hidden inside this ball?"

Repeat demonstration with the block and the eraser.

"How about this pomegranate? These peanuts?"

Open a peanut to show the inside.

"Could we see what was inside before we opened this? That's because it was 'hidden.' Sometimes words can hide things. How can we open words up to see what's inside? Let's look at the two words 'make me.'

Can anyone use them in a sentence? Now check how you feel when I say some of them to you: *You make me so upset. You make me so confused. You make me so worried.* Does anyone notice any feelings inside when I say that? What do you think is happening? Does it sound as if I am blaming you when I use these words?"

Continue: "If I'm feeling confused, do you enjoy hearing me say that you make me confused? Do you think I meant to blame you or to tell you about what's inside of me? In what way are the two words *make me* like this peanut?"

"If I feel upset, would you prefer that I say, *You make me so upset* or would you prefer that I own my feelings and say, without any hidden blame, *I feel upset?*"

To clarify, say more blaming phrases and ask students to translate these into feeling statements.

Example: "If I make the blaming statement, *You make me feel nervous,* how could I change that to own my feelings, using three little words?" (Translation: *I feel nervous.*)

More examples:

They make me embarrassed. (Translation: I feel embarrassed.)

He makes me (so) mad. (Translation: I feel mad.)

She makes me angry. (Translation: I feel angry.)

It worries me. (Translation: I feel worried.)

Variations and Extensions:

- Add what you might wish: *I feel nervous; I wish I could relax.*
- For a slight twist, change the phrase to *You embarrass me.* (Translation: *I feel embarrassed.)*
- Turn the situation around. In pairs, act it out so someone says to you, *You make me (so) nervous.* Guess their feeling: *Are you feeling nervous?*

Adapted from *Feelings, Wishes, Needs, Requests: The Big Book of Games and Activities That Promote Compassion and Community* by H. Holley Humphrey. Soaring Spirit Press, 233 Rogue River Hwy. #173, Grants Pass, OR 97527/ 541-862-2086.

Topic: Feelings

Title:	Owners Up-Seven Up
Objective:	To translate expressions of blame into expressions of feelings
Type of Activity:	Game (based on "Heads Up, Seven Up")
Group Size:	Entire Class
Space/Time:	Classroom with students at tables or desks/20+ minutes
Materials:	Pencils or pens, cardstock, index cards, or construction paper (laminate if possible)

Preparation:

Review concept of "owned" feelings versus "disowned" feelings. See activity titled *Three Little Words*. Use several examples so everyone is clear about the concept.

Copy the following phrases onto cards.

1. That makes me so
2. You make me so
3. They make me so
4. It makes me so
5. She makes me so
6. He makes me so
7. That makes me feel
8. You make me feel
9. They make me feel
10. It makes me feel

11. She makes me feel
12. He makes me feel
13. That hurt me when
14. He hurt my feelings when
15. They hurt me when
16. You hurt my feelings.

Procedure:

1. Ask students to sit at their desks with their heads down so they can't see anybody. They stick one thumb up to be chosen.
2. Seven people are selected to be "It," becoming the "Seven Up."
3. Each of the Seven Up group selects a card and walks around the room, deciding who to give it to. When they put the card down on someone's desk, they gently push that person's thumb down. The "thumb down" person is now one of the potential "owners."
4. A designated person says, "Owners Up-Seven Up." This means that the Seven Up group stands in the front of the room and the Owners stand by their desks. One at a time, Owners read their cards and translate them into ownership statements, then guess who gave it to them.

If they guess accurately, they become a member of the Seven Up group for the next game, and their tagger sits down. If they don't guess accurately, the person guessed simply says, "No, not I." The real person is not revealed and gets another turn as one of the Seven Up group.

Adapted from an exercise by Holly Humphrey.

Topic: Needs

Title:	Treasure Chests
Objective:	To identify and recognize the importance of values and needs
Type of Activity:	Art and writing
Group Size:	5–15
Space/Time:	Classroom/30 minutes
Materials:	Colored paper cut into jewel shapes, an envelope (treasure chest) for each child, art supplies such as glue, glitter, pens, foil

Procedure:

1. Introduce this activity by asking the whole class when they feel most joyous, happy, and/or satisfied. Write students' answers on the board. To stimulate thinking, ask students what they value in relationships, in themselves, in others, in nature, in school, at home, during free time, in life.
2. Suggest that our needs and values are like precious jewels in our life.
3. Ask them to write what they value on paper "jewels."
4. Give each student an envelope to decorate as a treasure chest for their jewels.
5. In a small or large group discussion, ask for volunteers to share their jewels.
6. Option: Survey the class for common needs and values, that everyone agrees are important. Make a class display of all the jewels.

Topic: Needs

Title:	Needs Collage
Objective:	To cultivate the habit of thinking in terms of needs
Type of Activity:	Art and writing
Group Size:	Entire Class, divided into pairs or small groups
Space/Time:	Tables to work on/30+ minutes
Materials:	Magazines, scissors, glue, markers, crayons, large chart paper for each pair or group

Procedure:

1. Review Needs List. (See Chapter 4.)
2. Work in pairs or small groups to find and cut out magazine pictures that depict a person's needs being met; also find pictures showing needs not being met.
3. Each group divides their chart paper in half, labeling one side, "Needs Met" and the other side "Needs Not Met."
4. Students paste their pictures in appropriate columns on their chart, and write the specific need(s) under each picture. (Option: Students may imagine both met and unmet needs in one picture and make a collage that represents both.)
5. When each pair or group is finished with their collage, they can share them with the whole class.

Variations and Extensions:

They can contribute their pictures to a large class collage.

Topic: Needs

Title:	FUN for You
Objective:	To see that we meet our need for fun in many different ways
Type of Activity:	Writing, discussion, drawing
Group Size:	Entire Class
Space/Time:	Adaptable
Materials:	Journals, pencils or pens

Procedure:

Questions for writing, discussion, drawing:

1. What's one thing you can do to meet your need for fun that: you can do alone? Takes less than one minute? Costs no money? You can do indoors on a rainy day?
2. What's one thing you have done to meet your need for fun today?
3. What's one thing you did for fun when you were younger?
4. What's one thing you'd like to do for fun during vacation?
5. When is learning the most fun for you?
6. What is the most fun you've ever had in school?
7. If fun were a color, what color would it be?
8. Find a person in your group who has fun doing something that you've never done.
9. Why is it helpful to know many ways to meet your need for fun?

10. How do you feel when your need for fun is being met?
11. How do you feel when your need for fun isn't being met?
12. How can you tell when you need to have some fun?
13. Tell about a time when someone was having fun in a way that made things hard for you or others.
14. Has anyone ever stopped you from having fun? What do you guess was their need for stopping you?
15. Have you ever made life more fun for someone? What did you do?

Topic: Needs

Title:	FUN Charts
Objective:	To see how people find different ways to meet the same needs
Type of Activity:	Small group discussion
Group Size:	Entire Class
Space/Time:	Room for small groups to work together/ 20+ minutes
Materials:	One handout with 2 columns titled, "EVERYONE in our group has fun doing this" and "SOME people in our group have fun doing this"; poster-size Needs List

Procedure:

1. Display a Needs List. (See Chapter 4.) Talk about our need for FUN.
2. Demonstrate for class: Sit in a circle with three volunteers. Say something like, One way I meet my need for fun is by swimming. Is that fun for you too? If everyone in your small group says, Yes, write "swimming" in the column on the handout labeled "EVERYONE in our group has FUN doing this." If anyone says, No, then write "swimming" in the column labeled, "SOME people in our group have fun doing this." Pass the handout to the person next to you. He says something that's fun for him and repeats the process.
3. Break into groups of 3–5 students each and ask them to follow your demonstration and fill in their chart. (Note: Ask them to think of ways they have fun that don't create problems for others.)
4. Meet back in a large circle to share what they noticed and what they learned in this activity.

Discussion Options:

- Make the statement: "We all have the same basic needs. However, the things we each choose to do to meet these needs may be different from what others choose." Ask for examples from their small groups.
- With students sitting next to the people who were in their group, pass a "talking object" around the circle and invite each student to say one thing she discovered by doing the activity.
- Write on the board, "We all have the need for fun, but we meet that need in different ways." Ask students if they agree or disagree with that statement. Ask them to support their answers with examples from their small groups.
- Use a Venn diagram (overlapping circles) to represent students by how they like to meet their need for fun.

Topic: Needs

Title:	Chain of Belonging
Objective:	To appreciate the many ways we meet our need for belonging
Type of Activity:	Discussion, writing, art
Group Size:	Entire Class
Space/Time:	Classroom/ongoing project
Materials:	Large poster of Needs, lots of strips of paper (1" x 9") in many colors, a legal size envelope for each student, glue, tape or stapler

Procedure:

1. Refer to the Basic Needs poster and review the need for belonging.
2. Sit in a circle and pass around a "talking object" to give each student an opportunity to say one way that people can meet their need for belonging. Point out that sharing in a circle is one way to meet this need.
3. Ask students to write on each strip of paper one way to meet the need for belonging. Ask them to leave a half-inch margin on each end so that the strips can be joined in a chain without covering the writing.
4. Make or post these suggestions:
   - Write the name of a friend and what you do together.
   - Write the name of a friend and draw a picture of what you do together.
   - Describe a group to which you belong.
   - Write something you choose to do to connect with others at school.

- Write about a little thing someone did that helped you meet your need to belong. For example, *She moved over to make room for me in the circle.*
- Write about something you did that helped someone else meet his need to belong.

5. Store strips in individual envelopes or one class envelope until you are ready to assemble the chain.
6. At the end of each day, allow time for reflection on what students did that day that helped them meet their need for belonging. Put these ideas on links and store them in an envelope until you are ready to assemble the chain.
7. After you have collected a lot of strips, assemble the chain and put it up in the room.
8. Celebrate how the need for belonging was met by everyone contributing to making the chain.

Topic: Whole Model

Title:	Matching Game
Objective:	To translate communication challenges into NVC expressions
Type of Activity:	Writing and interacting
Group Size:	At least 8
Space/Time:	Make statements on Day 1, play games on Day 2
Materials:	Paper, pencils to write a number of 4-step NVC statements, each step written on a separate index card

Example:	(one step per card)
Observation:	When you said "No"
Feeling:	I felt puzzled
Need:	I'd like to understand
Request:	Will you tell me why you said "No?"
	Make enough expressions for each student to have one card.

Procedure

1. Students tell about communication challenges they have experienced, including the basic context and situation.
2. The teacher or a group of volunteer students takes the situations, translates them into NVC statements (using the four steps: Observations, Feelings, Needs, Requests), and writes each step on a different card.
3. Shuffle the cards and ask each student to draw a card. Students move around the room trying to find the students who have the three other parts of their statement.
4. When all four members of a group find each other, each reads her 4-step expression to the entire group.

Topic: Whole Model

Title:	Stories
Objective:	To develop skills of making observations and guessing feelings, needs, and requests
Type of Activity:	Class discussion
Group Size:	Entire class: large or small groups
Space/Time:	Any
Materials:	Age-appropriate photos or illustrations of people. A book of photographs, such as *Lazy Man's Guide to Enlightenment*, can be used or photos from magazines
Preparation:	Familiarity with observations, feelings, needs, and requests

Procedure:

Students look at one photo and answer questions.

Observations:

What do you see happening?

How do you know that it is happening? Would a video camera see what you described?

Feelings:

What might the person or people be feeling?

How might you feel in this situation?

Needs:

What do you think needs are of the people in this picture?

What else could they be needing?

What needs would you have in this situation?

Requests:

What do you think a person in the picture would want to request?

What would the person say to make the request?

Variations and Extensions:

1. Put answers to questions on cards and display them on the bulletin board under the photos.
2. Small group activity: Each group chooses one picture and writes or tells a story about it, answering the questions, What happened before? and What is happening now? Write the rest of the story so that the identified needs are met.
3. Write or dictate journal entries inspired by the photos, as if you were one of the people in the photo. Identify feelings and needs and describe how the needs of the person get met. Story titles could be "Guess What Happened To Me Today?" or "How I Solved the Problem."
4. Use literature instead of photos in the same way: Talk with students about characters in literature, identifying their feelings and needs, and ways they attempt to meet their needs.

Topic: Listening

Title:	Four Ears
Objective:	• To increase choice about how we hear messages • To distinguish between hearing Jackal messages and hearing Giraffe messages
Type of Activity:	Roleplays
Group Size:	4–12 (divide into two groups if more than 12)
Space/Time:	Whole group sits in circle/20+ minutes
Materials:	A jackal puppet, two sets of giraffe ears and two sets of jackal ears—Paper ears or hand signals for ears can be used: hands on head, palms forward for jackal ears out and facing backward for jackal ears in; hands on heart, palms facing forward for giraffe ears out and facing backward for giraffe ears in.

See Resources page for ordering puppets and ears.

Procedure:

1. Explain the four distinctions: jackal and giraffe ears worn in and out. Jackal ears facing forward is blaming the outside world, and facing backward is blaming yourself. Giraffe ears facing forward is empathizing with the person's pain, facing backward is empathizing with your own pain.

2. Model the exercise by asking students, "What has someone said to you in the past that you didn't like hearing?"

   Respond in four ways, using the ears.

   Example: One student says, "That's an ugly shirt you're wearing."

   Response with jackal ears facing backward (self-critical):

   "I never should have worn this shirt; I have such poor taste."

Response with jackal ears facing forward (critical of others):

"You have terrible taste!"

Response with giraffe ears facing backwards (self-empathy):

"I feel irritated because I want to be respected for my choices."

Response with giraffe ears facing forward (empathy for others):

"Are you upset because you like a different style of clothes?"

Variation:

1. Hand out four sets of ears (2 giraffe, 2 jackal) evenly spaced around the circle.
2. Holding the jackal puppet, one person expresses a hard-to-hear statement such as, "Your answer is wrong."
3. Students wearing ears respond to the statement based on which ears they are wearing and the direction the ears are facing.
4. Ask students if they agree: "Does that sound like a jackal response or a giraffe response?"
5. When all four students have completed their responses ask them to pass ears to the left to give another four students opportunities to respond. The person with the jackal puppet passes it to his left and that student make a new hard-to-hear statement.

   Option: Make some statements that are fun to hear as well as some that are hard to hear. Make one of your statements a simple "No."

Topic: Listening

Title:	What Ears Are You Wearing?
Objective:	To experience more choice in how we listen
Type of Activity:	Scripted role-plays
Group Size:	Adapt for any size
Space/Time:	Space for circle seating/30 minutes
Materials:	Giraffe ears and jackal ears You can order ears or use hands to indicate ears: Use hands on head with palms forward or backward for the Jackal. Use hands on the heart with palms forward or backward for the Giraffe. Five colors of paper (red, green, blue, purple, yellow) cut into strips with one statement or response written on each. (See following pages.)

See Resources page for ordering puppets and ears.

Procedure:

1. Hand each student one of the strips of paper.
2. Beginning with the "red series" ask the student with the red "Statement" to read his script aloud.
3. Ask the student with the red #1 (R1) response to read it aloud.
4. Tell students that each of the response strips is either a jackal way of hearing or a giraffe way of hearing. Ask participants to put their hands on their heads or over their hearts to indicate whether they think it is a jackal or a giraffe way of hearing. [Jackal ears facing out is blaming the outside world and facing in is blaming yourself. Giraffe ears facing out is empathizing with the person's pain and facing in is empathizing with your pain.]
5. After seeing the response of the other students and perhaps after some discussion, the person who read the response puts on the appropriate ears.

6. Continue by asking the participant with the R2 response to read her response aloud and ask participants what kind of response they hear. The person who read the response puts on the appropriate ears. Continue until everyone has heard all red responses.

7. Repeat with other colored strips.

What Ears Are You Wearing? Scripts

Red slips:

(R Statement) Hurry up! Get your coat on. We're going to be late.

(R1 Response) You're so mean, making me do things I don't like.

(R2 Response) I have no choice. I'm like a slave.

(R3 Response) You want me to put my coat on now?

(R4 Response) Are you afraid that we will be late?

Green slips:

(G Statement) You spelled the word "house" wrong.

(G1 Response) You think you know it all.

(G2 Response) You want me to spell "house" the standard way?

(G3 Response) I'm so stupid.

(G4 Response) I can't spell. I'm never going to write again.

(G5 Response) I would like to know how to spell "house."

Blue slips:

(B Statement) You shouldn't be eating a snack now.

(B1 Response) You are not the boss of me.

(B2 Response) I'm always doing things wrong.

(B3 Response) You don't like me.

(B4 Response) Thanks, I forgot.

(B5 Response) Our class rule is to not eat snacks now.

(B6 Response) I'm afraid I will get punished.

(B7 Response) You are talking Jackal. You are wrong.

Purple slips:

(P Statement) You have to make a pie for our potluck.

(P1 Response) You would like me to make a pie.

(P2 Response) Who do you think you are, telling me what to do?

(P3 Response) I don't know what I'm going to do. I'm so stupid. I don't know how to make a pie.

(P4) I want to be able to choose what I bring to the potluck.

Yellow slips:

(Y Statement) Sit up straight and use good manners.

(Y1 Response) I can't ever do anything right. You hate me.

(Y2 Response) He's rude for saying that.

(Y3 Response) I want to enjoy my lunch without worrying about manners.

(Y4 Response) Do you want me to sit up because you're worried that I may not be accepted by others if I were to eat this way in their homes?

(Y5 Response) How mean of you to embarrass me in front of my friends.

Variations and Extensions:

- Have students make up the phrases and responses without using written scripts.

- Use positive statements, e.g. "You are so handsome!" or "Where did you get that beautiful hat?"

Topic: Listening

Title:	Empathy Role-plays
Objective:	To give and receive empathy
Type of Activity:	Empathic Dialogue
Group Size:	2–10
Space/Time:	Space for two to sit face to face/10 minutes minimum
Materials:	NVC chart or a prompt chart that says: What are they feeling? . . . What are they needing?
Preparation:	Introduction to feelings and needs and empathic listening

Demonstration Procedure:

Choose a person "B" to share something painful, scary, frustrating, or joyful. (An alternative is to ask her to choose a script written on a slip of paper.) Guess what the person might be feeling and needing.

Give several rounds of empathy.

Example:

B: People are so rude. At the end of class, they always push their way to the door.

A: Are you irritated and want more consideration for everyone in the class?

B: Yeah, I got knocked down a couple of times, too.

A: So it's scary besides? You want to be safe at school?

B: Yeah, they just don't care about anyone but themselves.

A: You're upset when you think people don't care about each other? Would you like people to care about others more?

B: Yeah, they just don't think about anything except getting out fast.

A: Would you like people to think about their actions and how they affect others before they act?

B: Yeah.

Optional: Guessing a request:

A: I wonder if you'd like to hear from others in the class whether they have similar feelings?

Reminders:

- Speaker "B" does not necessarily speak in Giraffe.
- It is not important for "A" to guess a feeling or need correctly. What is important is that "A" is interested in the other's feelings and needs.
- Empathy is not what you do or say but a way of being totally present for the person. You are not trying to figure them out or to be right.
- Suggest that speakers pause frequently to allow for empathy practice.
- If the person empathizing is confused about what she is hearing, she may need to interrupt the speaker and ask for clarification.

Procedure for practice:

Divide students into pairs. Student "B" expresses something that is triggering anger, fear, frustration, or happiness. "A" guesses "B's" feelings and needs. At the end, ask for feedback from all the dyads—how they felt about the role-play, what worked, and what did not work. Change roles so that "A" becomes "B" and "B" becomes "A," and continue.

Variations and Extensions:

Divide students into groups of three: one person expresses, one empathizes, and one observes. The person expressing doesn't try to use Giraffe Language. At the end, all three share what they noticed about the experience. Change roles until each person has played each role.

In larger groups, sit in a circle and recognize the person who wants to be listened to empathically. The others take turns guessing the feelings and needs. The guessing can be done "popcorn" style (anyone from anywhere in the room may offer a guess) or sequentially around the circle (anyone can "pass"). Evaluate the session at the end.

Reflection:

When a group empathy session is complete, first ask the person who was in pain to share what he noticed as well as how he felt during and after the session. Then, ask the person who gave empathy what he noticed and how he felt during and after the session. Last, ask the observers what they noticed and how they felt.

Topic: Anger

Title:	Red Flags
Objective:	To recognize anger as a signal of unmet needs
Type of Activity:	Discussion, art, and writing
Group Size:	5–15
Space/Time:	Classroom/20 minutes
Materials:	Chop sticks (one per person), red paper cut into flag shapes, tape

Procedure:

Note: This activity requires an understanding of needs and feelings and an ability to recognize when one is angry and to know how to calm or release anger in the body.

Discussion

1. Teacher: Share your understanding.
   Anger is a strong feeling mixed with thoughts. It is a 'red flag' warning us that the following might be going on:

   a) an important need is not being met;

   b) we are blaming someone for not meeting our need;

   c) we are about to do something that we will regret later.

2. Invite thoughts and feelings about the above statements.

3. Share your understanding about identifying feelings and needs.
   "We can take better care of ourselves if we release the other person from blame and identify our feelings and needs."

4. Invite reactions and feelings to the statement in #3 above.

5. "Underneath the anger there are other feelings, such as hurt, sadness, or fear. Think of a time when you were angry. Can you guess what feelings might have been underneath the anger?"

Activity:

Make Red Flags as reminders that underlying anger are strong feelings and needs that can be identified.

Fold red paper and tape it around a chop stick to make a flag. On one side of the flag, write:

> "I feel . . . because I need . . . "

Students can keep their flags in their desks to remind them to identify their feelings and needs beneath their anger.

Topic: Anger

Title:	Where Is the Anger?
Objective:	• To increase awareness of anger and how it manifests in the body • To increase ability to work with anger
Type of Activity:	Self-awareness and charting
Group Size:	Entire Class
Space/Time:	Room for a circle and room for coloring/20 minutes +
Materials:	Handout with the outline of a human body

Procedure:

1. Students stand or sit in a circle. Teacher says, "Take a few minutes to pay attention to your breath. What do you notice?"
   Allow 1–3 minutes.
2. "Think of a time when you were angry. Close your eyes. Now, take a few moments to remember the place, the people, and the reason you were angry. Notice what is happening in your body."
3. "Now open your eyes and, if you like, share about what you noticed."

   Possibilities: heart beating faster, face getting hot, eyes narrowing, stomach tightening, hands making fists, jaw clenching, feeling jumpy, wanting to move into action fast, etc.
4. Invite each person to draw on the body diagram what they felt and where they felt it. Students can use whatever colors and shapes make sense to them.
5. Share diagrams.

Topic: Anger

Title:	Anger Thermometer
Objective:	To increase awareness of anger and to experience how anger is defused when we identify the underlying feelings and needs
Type of Activity:	Discussion and charting
Group Size:	Any
Space/Time:	Classroom/20+ minutes for each session
Materials:	Anger Thermometer handout, pencils

Procedure:

Session 1

1. Ask students to: Think about a time when you were angry. How "hot" was your anger? Mark the level of "heat" you experienced in that situation on your Anger Thermometer.
2. Think of four different times when you have been angry. Write down these situations in as few words as possible and number them #1, #2, #3, and #4. Then mark on the thermometer with #1, #2, #3, #4 to indicate the relative heat of the anger you experienced in each situation. (Ask young children to think about one situation and mark the temperature with colors that express the heat of their anger-yellow, mild; orange, medium; red, hot.)

Session 2

1. After doing the activity: Translating Anger Into Feelings and Needs, ask the students to translate each of their four situations into feelings and needs.
2. Ask: How do you feel after translating your anger into feelings and needs? Where would you record your feelings, now, on the Anger Thermometer?

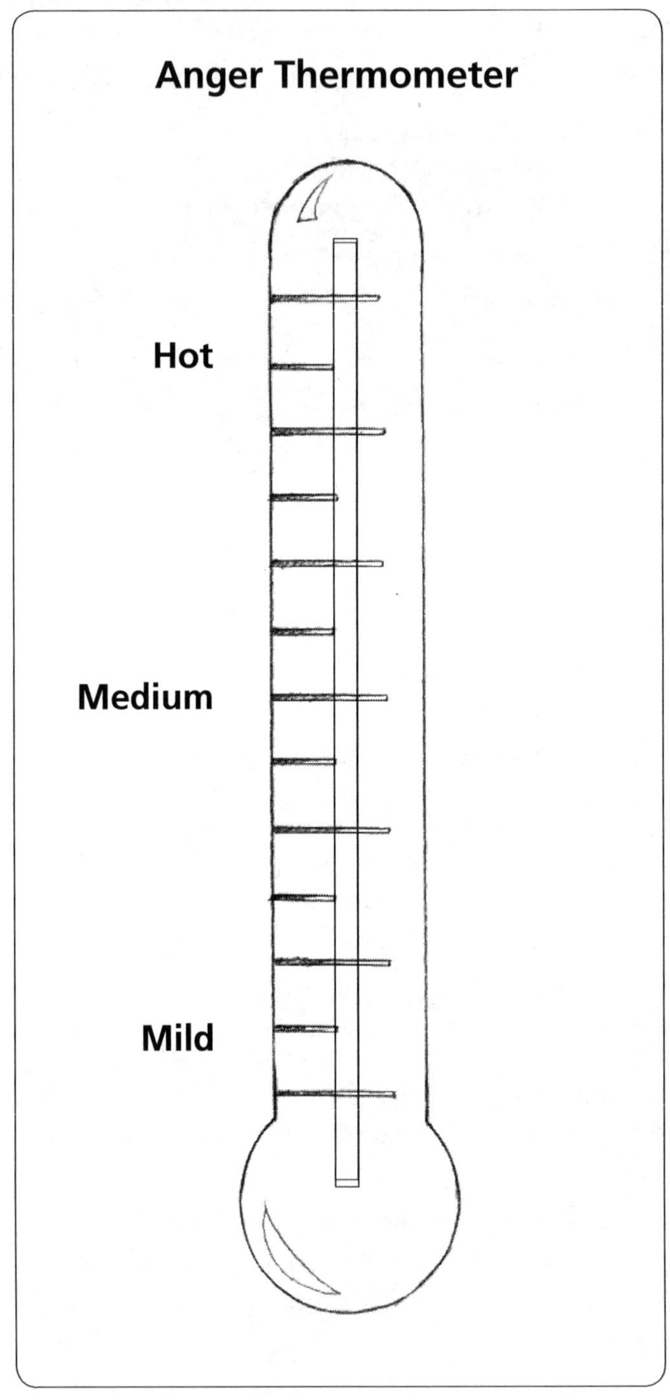
Anger Thermometer
Hot
Medium
Mild

Topic: Anger

Title:	Translating Anger Into Feelings and Needs
Objective:	To defuse anger by identifying the underlying feelings and needs
Type of Activity:	Discussion and written (or spoken) activity
Group size:	Any
Space/Time:	Classroom/20+ minutes
Materials:	Handouts (on following pages), pencils

Procedure:

1. Introduce the activity by asking the students to think about a time when they felt angry. List these situations on the blackboard, in as few words as possible. ("She said I was a creep." "He pushed me." "She gave me an F on my paper.") After writing 4–6 situations on the board, go back to the first situation and ask the person whose situation it was: "When this happened, what thoughts did you have?" Write the thoughts next to the situation. Do the same for each of the situations.

2. Discuss with the students what you and they notice about the kinds of thinking that accompany anger. Most often, these messages will include the thought that someone "should" have done things differently than they did, whether the word "should" is stated explicitly or implied. "Should" thinking includes moralistic labels such as right/wrong/good/bad, fair/unfair, appropriate/inappropriate. Point out that it is this kind of jackal thinking that is the cause of anger. Underneath the angry thoughts are feelings and needs. The feelings are most often hurt or fear. The needs will vary with the situation, but they are always needs that are important to us and that, in the particular situation, are not getting met.

3. Using the situations on the handout, or others from their own experience, help the students to identify their feelings and needs. Notice the difference when angry thoughts are absent.

Situations That Can Trigger Anger

I didn't get to go skating on the class field trip.

Feeling ______________________ Need ______________________

My friend's parents wouldn't let me stay over.

Feeling ______________________ Need ______________________

Someone said I cheated in a game.

Feeling ______________________ Need ______________________

Someone called me "stupid" in front of my friends.

Feeling ______________________ Need ______________________

Someone said my new shirt was "ugly."

Feeling ______________________ Need ______________________

I dropped the ball so my team lost the championship game.

Feeling ______________________ Need ______________________

Someone laughed when I fell down and hurt myself.

Feeling ______________________ Need ______________________

Kids on the playground said I couldn't play with them.

Feeling ________________ Need ________________

My grandmother died because she was ill from smoking.

Feeling ________________ Need ________________

I didn't get invited to a cool birthday party.

Feeling ________________ Need ________________

My parents yelled at me rather than talking to me.

Feeling ________________ Need ________________

My dog is really sick because someone gave him chocolate.

Feeling ________________ Need ________________

I couldn't finish my work because I didn't understand the assignment.

Feeling ________________ Need ________________

Topic: Daily Giraffe

Title:	The Tube of Communication
Objective:	• To be mindful of the flow of communication • To know when to express and when to listen
Type of Activity:	Demonstration and Roleplay
Group Size:	Any
Space/Time:	Classroom/20 minutes
Materials:	Clear plexiglass tube (1.5 inch diameter and 18–24" long) or a transparency rolled and taped in a tube shape, 2 different colored scarves, two 24" by .5" wooden dowels (or 2 chopsticks), role-play scripts

Procedure:

1. Demonstration: Use the "Tube of Communication" and scarves. Holding the tube to your eye, look through the tube. Make eye contact with each student to show that the tube is unobstructed. Imagine that one scarf represents your message. With a dowel, push it into one end of the tube while you express your message using "classical Giraffe Language": State your observations, feelings, needs, and request. When communication works well, we take turns talking back and forth like this. To demonstrate, put the other scarf in the tube and push it through going in the opposite direction.

2. Now imagine that someone reacts before you can send your message all the way through. Demonstrate, as you begin to talk, by pushing your scarf through and then stuff the other scarf/message into the other end of the tube. This is a verbal traffic jam. Neither person can get his/her message through to be heard by the other.

How to Get Out of a Verbal Traffic Jam:

3. If one person removes her scarf message from the tube and gives herself empathy then guesses the feelings and needs of the other, the tube will clear again. (Push the scarf through to demonstrate that the message has been successfully sent.) Once the tube is clear, the flow of communication changes and the first message can be re-sent. It may have changed a bit in the process from hearing the needs of the other. (Push the other scarf through to demonstrate a successful communication.)

4. The teacher demonstrates the pattern a few times: She sends an original message, interrupts, removes her scarf and offers empathy, has the other person resend his message, etc. Students work in pairs to manipulate the scarves while they role-play using their own messages.

Adapted from *Practice, Practice, Practice: An Illustrated Study Guide to Nonviolent Communication* by H. Holley Humphrey. Soaring Spirit Press, 233 Rogue River Hwy. #173, Grants Pass, OR 97527/ 541-862-2086.

Topic: Daily Giraffe

Title:	Role-plays
Objective:	• To experience the choices we have in how we express ourselves and how we listen to others • To practice the NVC process
Type of Activity:	Interactive, dramatic dialogue
Group Size:	Any
Space/Time:	Any
Materials:	Written role-plays or live situations, NVC chart of the 4 Steps (see Chapter 4)
Preparation:	Previous practice with the entire NVC process

Procedure:

1. Participant "A" defines the situation by stating:
   a. Her role: I have an older sister who stays in the bathroom a long time and won't let me in when I need to use it.
   b. The role she wants Participant "B" to take: You're my sister.
   c. The time and place of the dialogue, if relevant: It's this morning, ten minutes before I leave for school.
   d. An opening line or two for Participant B: My sister says, "Stop bothering me. You already had your turn."

Note: "A" may tell more of the story only if it's crucial to the role-play. Spend group time practicing rather than explaining the situation. During the role-play "A" can instruct "B" to make it more real: "No, my sister wouldn't say that; she'd probably say . . ."

2. "B" gives the opening lines and the play is under way. Usually "A" speaks Giraffe Language while "B" speaks Jackal Language.

   Options: If this doesn't work for "A," "A" can speak Jackal and "B" speaks Giraffe.

   Another option is for "B" to put on Giraffe ears and to give empathy to "A" until "A" is ready to give empathy to "B."

3. When the enactment ends or the prearranged ending time comes, give both "A" and "B" the opportunity to express what worked, what didn't work, and what they learned. Observers can then contribute what they saw and felt.

Variation:

Students may act out the scene in Jackal Language first and then with one person speaking Giraffe.

Topic: Daily Giraffe

See Resources page for ordering puppets and ears.

Title:	Mediation
Objective:	To learn how to mediate conflicts
Type of Activity:	Role-play
Group Size:	Any
Space/Time:	Any
Materials:	Giraffe puppet, giraffe ears
Demonstrate:	The procedure for mediating using puppet and ears
Set up:	Select three players One player is the mediator Two players are arguing Choose a conflict situation

Procedure:

1. The mediator gives one person a giraffe puppet and the other giraffe ears.
2. The mediator looks at the Giraffe speaker and says, "Facts" or "Observations."
3. The Giraffe speaker states the facts of the situation. The mediator translates or stops her if she starts to tell things other than facts about what happened.
4. The mediator says to Giraffe speaker, "Feelings," and the Giraffe speaker expresses the feelings that were stimulated by what happened.
5. The mediator says to Giraffe speaker, "Needs," and the Giraffe speaker expresses the unmet needs that gave rise to her feelings.

6. The mediator says to the person wearing the giraffe ears, "What facts did you hear?" and the person wearing the ears responds.
7. The mediator asks the Giraffe speaker, "Is that what you meant to say?" and Giraffe speaker responds with "Yes" or "No." If the Giraffe speaker responds, "No," then the mediator asks the speaker to state the facts again. The mediator checks with the person wearing the ears to find out what he heard. . . . They repeat this process until the speaker is heard to her satisfaction.
8. The mediator then asks the person wearing the ears, "What feelings and needs did you hear?" Then he responds.
9. The mediator asks the Giraffe speaker, "Did he get what you said?" and the Giraffe speaker responds.
10. The two players trade roles and props and repeat steps 3–9.
11. The mediator then asks if either party can think of a solution that would meet both of their needs.
12. If a solution is agreed upon, the mediator congratulates them.
13. If a mutually agreeable solution is not reached within the time frame allotted, schedule another time soon to continue the process.

After demonstrating the procedure, ask students to act out scenarios in front of the class.

Keep puppet and ears available for future opportunities to mediate.

Topic: Daily Giraffe

Title: Co-Creating Rules

Objective: To agree on ground rules for the classroom

When everyone who is affected by the rules participates in making them, several things happen that contribute to compassionate relationships. Everyone becomes a participant in the classroom. Everyone's needs are heard and considered. Everyone has an opportunity to practice participatory decision-making about something that affects them on a daily basis. Co-creating class rules generally meets student and teacher needs for participation, respect, consideration, and assurance that needs matter in the classroom.

By contrast, in the typical teacher-directed classroom, the needs of the teacher are more important than the needs of the students. The teacher sets the rules and also determines the consequences for breaking them. The teacher then becomes the police person, noting when transgressions occur and meting out punishments.

To Co-create Class Rules we begin by asking two questions, either in class discussion or in a Council: "What kind of a classroom do you want? What do you need to feel safe enough to be yourself?"

Needs most often expressed are: safety, learning, respect, consideration for others, and care for the environment. Once a list of needs is generated, students can list some behaviors that would help meet those needs.

So what happens when someone in the class does something that doesn't meet the needs expressed by the class? There are several possibilities:

- Anyone can express what they observe, what needs are not met for them, and what they request.
- Anyone can make the request, "Would you be willing to find someone to give you empathy for your unmet needs?"
- Students can create a Self-Empathy Corner that they can go to—their choice—when they want to take some time to reconnect with their needs.
- Students can ask someone for empathy.

Topic: Daily Giraffe

Title:	A Show of Cards
Objectives:	• Learn feelings and needs vocabulary • Identify feelings and needs
Type of Activity:	Check-in
Group Size:	Entire Class
Space/Time:	Classroom
Materials:	Feelings and Needs cards (See next page.)

Procedure:

1. Photocopy ten Feelings cards and ten Needs cards for each student. Heavy paper or card stock is recommended.
2. Ask students to write one feeling on the back of each Feelings Card, and one need on the back of each Needs Card.
3. Throughout the day, the teacher asks for a show of cards to find out 1) how students are feeling, and 2) what needs are or are not being met by whatever is happening.

Option:

Students color their cards.

Students continue to add cards to their decks.

Variations:

1. Students ask for a show of cards.
2. When students arrive at school, they select Feelings and Needs Cards and place them on their desks so others can better understand "how they really are."

Feelings Cards

Needs Cards

Topic: Daily Giraffe

Title: Council

Objective:
- To give everyone in the class an opportunity to express and be heard
- To give everyone opportunities to listen
- To tap into the wisdom of the group

A form of Council has been practiced throughout the world in cultures that value equality, interdependence, honesty, respect, and community. Council begins with sitting in a circle so that each person can be seen and can see everyone else in the circle. Each person has an opportunity to speak. Most often a talking stick is passed to identify the speaker. When a person speaks, everyone else listens. Guidelines for the speaker are to speak briefly and from the heart. Those who are not speaking are counselled to listen attentively and deeply to what the speaker is expressing. In a classroom, Council can be a powerful way to meet needs for inclusion, understanding, connection, and for practice in speaking and listening from the heart.

In student groups, Councils have been used to check in with each person by sharing current feelings and needs. Councils are also used to share responses 1) to a subject that the class is studying, 2) to a situation at school, or 3) to a world event. Anyone can call a Council to address a specific topic.

One popular variation of the basic form of Council is called a Fishbowl. One small group of students forms a circle within a larger outer circle of listeners. Only the students in the inner circle talk, giving those in the outer circle an opportunity to listen deeply. This form was used in a class of fifth graders in Carpinteria, California. First the girls formed the inner circle and took turns speaking about what they found challenging and what they found fun about entering puberty. The boys listened. Later the boys formed the inner circle and shared what was difficult and fun for them about entering puberty while the girls listened. Then they all formed one circle and shared what they heard and what they learned. Students said that, after listening to each other, they understood each other better and appreciated each other's challenges more.

Topic: Daily Giraffe

Title:	Giraffe Notes
Objective:	To develop skills in composing, writing, and delivering a giraffe appreciation
Type of Activity:	Writing
Group Size:	Any
Space/Time:	15 minutes to present
Materials:	Giraffe Note forms (See next page.)
Preparation:	Familiarity with observations, feelings, needs, requests

Procedure:

1. Introduce the Giraffe Notes by asking each student to think of something that someone did that met a need for them.
2. Demonstrate filling out the Giraffe Note expressing appreciation.
3. Students write a Giraffe Note and deliver it.
4. Students can share how they feel after writing the note, and what needs were met. They can also share how it feels to receive a note and what needs are met by receiving appreciation from someone in the class.

Giraffe Note of Appreciation

When I think about…

I feel…

Because it meets my need for…

Chapter 6
A Guide to Lesson Planning

We wrote this book with educators in mind—teachers, administrators, counselors, school staff, and home school parents—to help you develop in your students genuine self-esteem, consideration for others, cooperation, and eagerness to learn. Knowing how much time is usually spent in classrooms disciplining students, we also wanted to provide you with proven ways to have fewer "discipline problems."

Although the examples we use are most typical of life and learning in elementary classrooms, we know from our experience that the principles and skill set we share in this book are equally relevant to middle school, high school, college students, and adults. We wrote the exercises with broad strokes to leave room for you to adapt them to your teaching/learning situation.

We have added this section, A Guide to Lesson Planning, to help you easily create lesson plans from the information and exercises in this book. Once again, these are broad strokes that can be refined for you, your students, your time schedule, and your curriculum. The following Lesson Plan suggestions can be translated into many processing modalities, including: discussing in large groups, small groups, dyads and triads; drawing pictures and sharing them orally; drawing pictures and writing about them; making up role-plays and skits; writing journals, essays, articles, and letters, etc.

Lesson Plan Suggestions

Section I: The Relationship-Teaching-Learning Connection

Chapter 1: Creating Safety and Trust shows how to establish emotional safety and trust in a learning environment.

At the beginning of the school year:

- Discuss the importance of safety and trust and the difference between physical and emotional safety.
- In a variety of ways, explore the information in Chapter 1 with students. They are likely to be fascinated to know what happens physiologically when they don't feel physically and emotionally safe.
- Students identify where and with whom they feel safe.
- Create Group Agreements: As a group, make a mutually determined agreement to replace teacher determined class rules.
  - * Work with students to discuss and mutually determine a list of things everyone in the class would like in order to create physical and emotional safety.
  - * Teachers: It is important that you include on the list behaviors that contribute to your safety, too.
  - * Elicit a list of agreements about the things students are willing to do to ensure safety for themselves and each other.
  - * Ask students to make this list into a poster and put it on a wall where it can be seen easily. Everyone can refer to it throughout the year and revise it as desired.

    (In some classrooms Group Agreements are signed by all of the class members.)

    (See page 168: Chapter 5, Daily Giraffe, Co-Creating Rules.)

Chapter 2: Relationships in the Classroom provides an opportunity to take a close look at what you, as the teacher, do now in your classroom and what you want to do in the future. The checklist-like format helps you take stock of four kinds of classroom relationships: you with yourself, you with your students, your students with each other, and your students with themselves and their learning. This chapter gives many suggestions for how to strengthen these relationships.

> **Student-Student Relationships:** Now that students have talked about safety and trust and have determined the interactions they need to feel physically and emotionally safe, the section called Student-Student Relationships can be used to stimulate thinking and discussion about how they actually interact with one another. This section gives numerous additional ideas for creating compassionate interactions in the classroom.

Make each of the subheadings in this section into a separate lesson:

- How do students share their gifts with one another?
- How do students communicate their feelings and needs?
- Do students make requests of others or do they make demands?
- How often do students make decisions about their learning and life in the classroom?
- To what extent to students learn together and from one another?
- Do students have a variety of forums to express themselves and hear others?

Student-Learning Relationships: This section brings to students' awareness their relationship to their learning process and shows them ways to enliven and take increasing responsibility for what and how they learn.

Make each of the subheadings in this section into a separate lesson:

- Do students know what their interests, talents and learning styles are?
- Are students actively engaged in their learning?
- Are students involved in setting learning objectives?
- Are students involved in evaluating their learning?
- Do teacher evaluations of students' work contribute to their learning process?
- How do students relate to mistakes and/or failures?
- To what extent is the study of human life connected to the community, to all other life forms, the biosphere, and the planet?
- Do students make meaningful connections with the curriculum?

Section II: Tools and Resources for Co-creating a Compassionate Classroom With Young People

Chapter 3: Rediscover Your Giving and Receiving Nature develops five premises that serve as a framework for a compassionate classroom and that underlie the process of Nonviolent Communication. These premises invite students to consider and question their assumptions about relating to themselves and others. The premises and exercises are likely to stimulate discussion and insight. Each of these premises has several exercises to support learning.

- Make each of the subheadings under each premise into a lesson. Many of the subheadings include exercises to assist you in quickly creating lesson plans.

  Depending on the needs of your students, the Premises could be presented in a different order than presented in the book.

  (See an Overview of the Premises and their subheadings on pages 44–45.)

- Ask students to make a poster of needs to put on a wall where everyone can see it. (See example on page 90.)
- Ask students to make a poster of feelings to put on a wall where everyone can see it. (See example on page 87.)
- Introduce the activity called Daily Giraffe: A Show of Cards on page 169.

Chapter 4: Relearn the Language of Giving and Receiving provides skill development for learning to listen and express effectively and compassionately with oneself and with one another.

- Use each of the bold headings in this chapter to create 3–4 lessons. Bold headings include: Intention, The Flow of Communication, Observations, Feelings, Anger, Needs, Requests, Listening to Myself: Self-Empathy, and Listening to Others: Empathy.

  Use the games and activities on Observations, Feelings, Needs, Listening, Anger and Whole Model in Chapter 5 to supplement your lessons.

- Ask students to discuss and make a What Language Are You Using? poster similar to the one on page 99. Encourage them to add their own ideas to each side of the chart.

- Ask students to discuss and make wall charts similar to the Giraffe Expressing and Giraffe Listening/Empathy charts on pages 80–81.

- For young students, make photocopies of the Giraffe Note of Appreciation on page 174. Have a stack of them in the classroom and help students find as many occasions as possible to use them. Some students may want to design their own notes.

Chapter 5: Develop Skills Through Activities and Games has teacher-tested and recommended games and activities to support learning. There is a table of contents for them on page 116. Many of the activities can be modified to support this learning for students of all ages.

Appendices

References

SECTION I

CHAPTER ONE

1. Alfie Kohn, *No Contest: The Case Against Competition*, Houghton Mifflin Company, 1992.

2 Daniel Goleman, *Emotional Intelligence*, Bantam, 1995.

3 Vilma Costetti, *Nonviolent Communication: Experimental Project in Primary Schools*, 2000.

4 James Garbarino and Ellen deLara, *And Words Can Hurt Forever: How to Protect Adolescents from Bullying, Harassment, and Emotional Violence*, Free Press, 2002.

5 Daniel Goleman, *Emotional Intelligence*, Bantam, 1995. Alfie Kohn, *Beyond Discipline*, Association for Supervision & Curriculum Development, 1996.

6 Daniel Goleman, *Emotional Intelligence*, Bantam, 1995.

7 Joseph Chilton Pearce, "Introduction," in Doc Lew Childre, *Teaching Children to Love*, Planetary Publications, 1996.

8 Doc Lew Childre, *Teaching Children to Love*, Planetary Publications, 1996.

9 Janet L. Surrey, "Relationship and Empowerment," *Work in Progress*, Stone Center Working Papers Series.

10 William Glasser, *The Quality School*, Harper Perennial, 1992. *The Quality School Teacher*, Harper Perennial, 1993.

11 Abraham Maslow, *Toward a Psychology of Being*, Van Nostrand, 1962.

12 William Glasser, 1992, 1993.

13 Virginia Satir, *PeopleMaking*, Science & Behavior Books, Inc., 1972.

CHAPTER TWO

1 Parker Palmer, *The Courage to Teach: Exploring the Inner Landscape of a Teacher's Life*, Jossey-Bass Publishers, 1998.

2 Mary Parker Follett, *Creative Experience*, Longmans Green, 1924. Mary Parker Follett, *Dynamic Administration*, Harper & Brothers, 1942.

3 Janet L. Surrey, "Relationship and Empowernment," *Work in Progress*, Stone Center Working Papers Series.

4 Marshall B. Rosenberg, *Life-Enriching Education*, PuddleDancer Press, 2003.

5 Riane Eisler, *Tomorrow's Children: A Blueprint for Partnership Education in the 21st Century*, Westview Press, 2000.

6 Personal communication with Marianne Gothlin, 2002.

7 Personal communication with Marianne Gothlin, 2002.

8 Alfie Kohn, *Beyond Discipline*, Association for Supervision & Curriculum Development, 1996.

9 Personal communication with Marianne Gothlin, 2002.

10 Marshall B. Rosenberg, 2003.

11 J. Krishnamurti, *Education and the Significance of Life*, Harper & Row, 1953. J. Krishnamurti, *On Education*, Harper & Row, 1974. William Glasser, 1992 & 1993. Alfie Kohn, 1996. Carl Rogers, *Freedom to Learn*, Charles E. Merrill, 1969. Carl Rogers, *On Personal Power*, Delacorte, 1977. John Dewey, *Experience and Education*, Touchstone Books, 1997.

12 Mariaemma Willis and Victoria Kindle Hodson, *Discover Your Child's Learning Style*, Prima Publishing, 1999.

SECTION II

CHAPTER THREE

1 Alfie Kohn, *The Brighter Side of Human Nature*, Basic Books, 1990.

2 Red and Kathy Grammer, "See Me Beautiful," in Teaching Peace (music CD), RedNote Records, 1986.

Resources

Books on Nonviolent Communication for Educators

Life-Enriching Education:
Nonviolent Communication Helps Schools Improve Performance, Reduce Conflict, and Enhance Relationships,
Marshall B. Rosenberg

Marshall Rosenberg presents a radical approach to education, showing how teachers, students, and administrators can apply the principles of Nonviolent Communication to create extraordinary schools that solve the complex problems facing schools today.

PuddleDancer Press, Fall 2003

Nonviolent Communication: A Language of Life, 2nd Edition
Marshall B. Rosenberg

PuddleDancer Press, 2003

A complete presentation of the Nonviolent Communication process, clarified and illustrated through stories, exercises, and dialogues.

Order at www.cnvc.org or 1-800-255-7696.

Parenting From Your Heart:
Sharing the Gifts of Compassion, Connection, and Choice
Inbal Kashtan

PuddleDancer Press, 2004

A 48-page booklet that addresses the challenges of parenting with real-world solutions for creating family relationships that meet everyone's needs.

Order at www.cnvc.org or 1-800-255-7697.

Teaching Children Compassionately:
How Students and Teachers Can Succeed With Mutual Understanding
Marshall B. Rosenberg

PuddleDancer Press, 2004

A 48-page booklet taken from a keynote address and workshop given to a national conference of Montessori educators.

Order at www.cnvc.org or 1-800-255-7697.

Raising Children Compassionately:
Parenting the Nonviolent Communication Way
Marshall B. Rosenberg

A 36-page booklet filled with insights and stories to support people who want to nurture children and themselves.

Order at www.cnvc.org or 1-800-255-7696.

The Mayor of Jackal Heights
Rita Herzog and Kathy Smith

An illustrated story—for children of all ages—about a boy mayor who begins to learn how to tame his town full of jackals with the help of his wise friend, Giraffe.

Order at www.cnvc.org or 1-800-255-7696.

Games for Speaking Compassion:
Fun Ways to Teach Nonviolent Communication to Kids
H. Holley Humphrey

Empathy Magic Press, 2004.

Order at www.empathymagic.com or 1-541-862-2043.

Compassionate Communication and Waldorf Schools
John Cunningham

This booklet has a dual purpose: to introduce the practice of Compassionate (Nonviolent) Communication to those interested in Waldorf education, and to provide a useful resource for learning this process.

To order, visit www.empathy-conexus.com.

NVC Classroom Materials

The No-Fault Zone Game
created by Sura Hart and Victoria Kindle Hodson

Makes use of a map and card decks to guide you, step by step, to the clarity, understanding, and connection you want—within yourself and with others. It makes conversations visible, tangible, and fun for ages 5–95. Available from www.TheNoFaultZone.com

Nonviolent Communication for Educators
(audiotape) by Marshall Rosenberg
(formerly *Nonviolent Communication: A Language of the Heart*)

Marshall Rosenberg's Keynote Address to the 1999 National Conference of Montessori Educators. Order from CNVC at www.cnvc.org or 1-800-255-7696.

Giraffe and Jackal puppets and ears
can be ordered from CNVC at www.cnvc.org or 1-800-255-7696.

Feeling Detours Board Game,
created by Marlene Marskornick

A fun way for players (ages 9+) to practice making distinctions between feelings and "feeling detours" such as, "I feel attacked," "I feel they are being rude," "You make me mad." Everything you need to "manufacture" this game is available on disk: game board, cards, guidebook, directions for playing. Contact marlenem@fidalgo.net.

Recommended Websites

Center for Nonviolent Communication
www.cnvc.org

Information about NVC trainings and projects worldwide is posted and updated on the website, along with NVC books, audiotapes and videos. You will also find contact information for regional NVC groups and for individual trainers around the world.

PuddleDancer Press

www.NonviolentCommunication.com

Our website helps you conveniently find and purchase our publications online, has detailed information about each of the publications we offer, support for PR and marketing efforts related to NVC, details of Marshall Rosenberg's background, ideas, and FAQs, Press related materials for producers and journalists, information about PuddleDancer Press and how to work with us, additional Resources including articles, reading lists, foreign rights publishing info, and more!

The No-Fault Zone

www.TheNoFaultZone.com

Victoria Kindle Hodson and Sura Hart, authors of *The Compassionate Classroom: Relationship Based Teaching and Learning,* offer workshops for educators and parents on Creating Compassionate Classrooms, Creating Compassionate Homes, and Conflict Resolution.

Partnership Education

www.partnershipway.org

Based on Riane Eisler's book *Tomorrow's Children,* Partnership Education provides a large frame for designing curriculum that promotes tolerance, understanding of our interconnectedness, and partnership relationships.

World Core Curriculum

www.unol.org/rms

World Core Curriculum offers a vast curricular frame, educating young people about their place in time and space—in families, local cultures, the world environment, and the universe.

Educators for Social Responsibility

www.esrnational.org

ESR offers well-tested curriculum materials and teacher training programs focusing on issues of social justice and peacemaking.

Recommended Reading

Bucciarelli, Deirdre and Sarah Pirtle (Eds.). *Partnership Education in Action*. Center for Partnership Studies, 2001.

Childre, Doc Lew. *Teaching Children to Love*. Planetary Publications, 1996.

Clark, Edward T. *Designing and Implementing an Integrated Curriculum: A Student-Centered Approach*. Holistic Education Press, 1997.

Eisler, Riane. *Tomorrow's Children: A Blueprint for Partnership Education in the 21st Century*. Westview Press, 2000.

Eisler, Riane and Ron Miller (Eds.). *Educating for Cultures of Peace*. Heinemann, 2004.

Faber, Adele and Elaine Mazlish. *How to Talk So Kids Will Listen, and How to Listen So Kids Will Talk*. Avon Books, 1980.

Fritz, Robert. *The Path of Least Resistance: Learning to Become the Creative Force in Your Own Life*. Fawcett Columbine, 1989.

Gatto, John Taylor. *Dumbing Us Down*. New Society Publishers, 1992.

Gatto. *A Different Kind of Teacher: Solving the Crisis of American Schooling*. Berkeley Hills Books, 2001.

Glasser, William. *The Quality School*. Harper Perennial, 1992.

Glasser. *The Quality School Teacher*. Harper Perennial, 1993.

Glazer, Steven (Ed.). *The Heart of Learning: Spirituality in Education*. Jeremy P. Tarcher/Putnam, 1999.

Goleman, Daniel. *Emotional Intelligence*. Bantam Books, 1995.

Gordon, Thomas. *T.E.T.: Teacher Effectiveness Training*. David McKay Company, Inc., 1974.

Hart, Sura and Marianne Gothlin. "Lessons from the Skarpnacks Free School." *Encounter: Education for Meaning and Social Justice*, Volume 15, Number 3, Autumn 2002.

Hodson, Victoria Kindle and Mariaemma Willis. *Discover Your Child's Learning Style*. Prima, 1999.

Hooks, Bell. *Teaching to Transgress: Education as the Practice of Freedom*. Routledge, 1994.

Koegel, Rob. "Learning to Partner with My Students." *Encounter: Education for Meaning and Social Justice*, Volume 15, Number 3, Autumn 2002.

Koegel, Rob and Ron Miller. "The Heart of Holistic Education: A Reconstructed Dialogue Between Ron Miller and Rob Koegel." *Encounter: Education for Meaning and Social Justice*, Volume 16, Number 2, Summer 2003.

Kohn, Alfie. *No Contest*. Houghton Mifflin Company, 1986.

Kohn. *The Brighter Side of Human Nature*. Basic Books, 1990.

Kohn. *Punished By Rewards*. Houghton Mifflin Company, 1993.

Kohn. *Beyond Discipline*. Association for Supervision and Curriculum Development, 1996.

Kreisberg, Seth. *Transforming Power: Domination, Empowerment, and Education*. State University of New York Press, 1992.

Krishnamurti, J. *Education and the Significance of Life*. Harper & Row, 1953.

Krishnamurti. *On Education*. Harper & Row, 1974.

Lantieri, Linda (Ed.). *Schools with Spirit: Nurturing the Inner Lives of Children and Teachers*. Beacon Press, 2001.

Lantieri, Linda and Janet Patti. *Waging Peace in Our Schools*. Beacon Press, 1996.

Miller, Ron (Ed.). *Creating Learning Communities: Models, Resources, and New Ways of Thinking About Teaching and Learning*. The Foundation for Educational Renewal, Inc., 2000.

Noddings, Nel. *The Challenge to Care in Schools: An Alternative Approach to Education*. Teachers College Press, Teachers College, Columbia University, 1993.

Noddings. *Starting at Home: Caring and Social Policy*. University of California Press, 2002.

Ohanian, Susan. *One Size Fits Few*. Heinemann, 1999.

Palmer, Parker J. *The Courage to Teach: Exploring the Inner Landscape of a Teacher's Life*. Jossey-Bass Publishers, 1998.

Pearce, Joseph Chilton. *The Biology of Transcendence*. Park Street Press, 2002.

Rogers, Carl R. *A Way of Being*. Houghton Mifflin Company, 1980.

Rosenberg, Marshall. *Nonviolent Communication, A Language of Life, 2nd Edition*. PuddleDancer Press, 2003.

Rosenberg. *Life-Enriching Education: Nonviolent Communication Helps Schools Improve Performance, Reduce Conflict, and Enhance Relationships*. PuddleDancer Press, 2003.

Rosenberg. *Raising Children Compassionately: Parenting the Nonviolent Communication Way*. Center for Nonviolent Communication, 2000.

Satir, Virginia. *Peoplemaking*. Behavior Books, Inc., 1972.

Special Issue on Partnership Education and Nonviolent Communication. *Encounter: Education for Meaning and Social Justice*, Volume 15, Number 3, Autumn 2002.

Wright, Esther. *Good Morning Class—I Love you!: Teaching from the Heart*. Jalmar Press, 1989.

Index

The No-Fault Classroom

Tools to Resolve Conflict & Foster Relationship Intelligence
by Sura Hart and Victoria Kindle Hodson
$17.95 — Trade Paper 8.5x11, 256pp
ISBN: 978-1-892005-18-2

Students Can Resolve Their Own Conflicts!

Offering far more than discipline techniques that move aggressive behavior out of the classroom to the playground or sidewalk, *The No-Fault Classroom* leads students ages 7–12 to develop skills in problem solving, empathic listening, and conflict resolution that will last a lifetime.

The book's twenty-one interactive and step-by-step lessons, construction materials, and adaptable scripts give educators the tools they need to return order and co- operation to the classroom and jumpstart engaged learning—from the rural school to the inner city, the charter school, to the home school classroom. *Curricular Tie-ins* guide teachers to use the conflict resolution tools they've developed to meet state learning requirements in social studies, language arts, history, reading, and science.

Respectful Parents, Respectful Kids

7 Keys to Turn Family Conflict Into Co-operation
by Sura Hart and Victoria Kindle Hodson
$17.95 — Trade Paper 7.5x9.25, 256pp
ISBN: 978-1-892005-22-9

Stop the Struggle—Find the Co-operation and Mutual Respect You Want!

Do more than simply correct bad behavior—finally unlock your parenting potential. Use this handbook to move beyond typical discipline techniques and begin creating an environment based on mutual respect, emotional safety, and positive, open communication. *Respectful Parents, Respectful Kids* offers *7 Simple Keys* to discover the mutual respect and nurturing relationships you've been looking for.

Life-Enriching Education

Nonviolent Communication Helps Schools Improve Performance, Reduce Conflict, and Enhance Relationships
by Marshall B. Rosenberg, PhD
$15.95 — Trade Paper 6x9, 192pp
ISBN: 978-1-892005-05-2

Filled with insight, adaptable exercises, and role-plays, *Life-Enriching Education* gives educators practical skills to generate mutually respectful classroom relationships. Discover how our language and organizational structures directly impact student potential, trust, self-esteem, and student enjoyment in their learning. Rediscover the joy of teaching in a classroom where each person's needs are respected!

Available from PuddleDancer Press, the Center for Nonviolent Communication, all major bookstores, and Amazon.com. Distributed by Independent Publisher's Group: 800-888-4741.

Save an extra 10% at NonviolentCommunication.com with code: **bookads**

Nonviolent Communication: A Language of Life, *Second Edition*

Life-Changing Tools for Healthy Relationships

Marshall B. Rosenberg, PhD

$19.95 — Trade Paper 6x9, 240pp

ISBN: 978-1-892005-03-8

What is "Violent" Communication?

If "violent" means acting in ways that result in hurt or harm, then much of how we communicate—judging others, bullying, having racial bias, blaming, finger pointing, discriminating, speaking without listening, criticizing others or ourselves, name-calling, reacting when angry, using political rhetoric, being defensive or judging who's "good/bad" or what's "right/wrong" with people—could indeed be called "violent communication."

What is "Nonviolent" Communication?
Nonviolent Communication is the integration of 4 things:

Consciousness: a set of principles that support living a life of empathy, care, courage, and authenticity
Language: understanding how words contribute to connection or distance
Communication: knowing how to ask for what we want, how to hear others even in disagreement, and how to move toward solutions that work for all
Means of influence: sharing "power with others" rather than using "power over others"

Speak Peace in a World of Conflict

What You Say Next Will Change Your World

by Marshall B. Rosenberg, PhD

$15.95 — Trade Paper 5-3/8x8-3/8, 208pp

ISBN: 978-1-892005-17-5

International peacemaker, mediator, and healer, Marshall Rosenberg shows you how the language you use is the key to enriching life. *Speak Peace* is filled with inspiring stories, lessons, and ideas drawn from more than forty years of mediating conflicts and healing relationships in some of the most war-torn, impoverished, and violent corners of the world. Find insight, practical skills, and powerful tools that will profoundly change your relationships and the course of your life for the better.

Being Genuine

Stop Being Nice, Start Being Real

by Thomas d'Ansembourg

$17.95 — Trade Paper 5-3/8x8-3/8, 280pp

ISBN: 978-1-892005-21-2

Being Genuine brings Thomas d'Ansembourg's blockbuster French title to the English market. His work offers you a fresh new perspective on the proven skills offered in the bestselling book, *Nonviolent Communication: A Language of Life*. Drawing on his own real-life examples and stories, Thomas d'Ansembourg provides practical skills and concrete steps that allow us to safely remove the masks we wear, which prevent the intimacy and satisfaction we desire with our intimate partners, children, parents, friends, family, and colleagues.

Based on Marshall Rosenberg's Nonviolent Communication process

Available from PuddleDancer Press, the Center for Nonviolent Communication, all major bookstores, and Amazon.com. Distributed by Independent Publisher's Group: 800-888-4741.

Save an extra 10% at NonviolentCommunication.com with code: **bookads**

Trade Booklets From PuddleDancer Press

Being Me, Loving You: *A Practical Guide to Extraordinary Relationships* **by Marshall B. Rosenberg, PhD** • Watch your relationships strengthen as you learn to think of love as something you "do," something you give freely from the heart. 80pp • **$6.95**

Getting Past the Pain Between Us: *Healing and Reconciliation Without Compromise* **by Marshall B. Rosenberg, PhD** • Learn simple steps to create the heartfelt presence necessary for lasting healing to occur—great for mediators, counselors, families, and couples. 48pp • **$6.95**

Graduating From Guilt: *Six Steps to Overcome Guilt and Reclaim Your Life* **by Holly Michelle Eckert** • The burden of guilt leaves us stuck, stressed, and feeling like we can never measure up. Through a proven six-step process, this book helps liberate you from the toxic guilt, blame, and shame you carry. 96pp • **$9.95**

Humanizing Health Care: *Creating Cultures of Compassion With Nonviolent Communication* **by Melanie Sears, RN, MBA** • Leveraging more than 25 years nursing experience, Melanie demonstrates the profound effectiveness of NVC to create lasting, positive improvements to patient care and the health care workplace. 112pp • **$9.95**

Parenting From Your Heart: *Sharing the Gifts of Compassion, Connection, and Choice* **by Inbal Kashtan** • Filled with insight and practical skills, this booklet will help you transform your parenting to address every day challenges. 48pp • **$6.95**

Raising Children Compassionately: *Parenting the Nonviolent Communication Way* **by Marshall B. Rosenberg, PhD** • Learn to create a mutually respectful, enriching family dynamic filled with heartfelt communication. 32pp • **$7.95**

The Surprising Purpose of Anger: *Beyond Anger Management: Finding the Gift* **by Marshall B. Rosenberg, PhD** • Marshall shows you how to use anger to discover what you need, and then how to meet your needs in more constructive, healthy ways. 48pp • **$6.95**

Teaching Children Compassionately: *How Students and Teachers Can Succeed With Mutual Understanding* **by Marshall B. Rosenberg, PhD** • In this national keynote address to Montessori educators, Marshall describes his progressive, radical approach to teaching that centers on compassionate connection. 48pp • **$6.95**

We Can Work It Out: *Resolving Conflicts Peacefully and Powerfully* **by Marshall B. Rosenberg, PhD** • Practical suggestions for fostering empathic connection, genuine co-operation, and satisfying resolutions in even the most difficult situations. 32pp • **$7.95**

What's Making You Angry? *10 Steps to Transforming Anger So Everyone Wins* **by Shari Klein and Neill Gibson** • A powerful, step-by-step approach to transform anger to find healthy, mutually satisfying outcomes. 32pp • **$7.95**

Available from www.NonviolentCommunication.com, www.CNVC.org, Amazon.com and all bookstores. Distributed by IPG: 800-888-4741

Save an extra 10% at NonviolentCommunication.com with code: **bookads**

About the Authors

Sura Hart and **Victoria Kindle Hodson** are co-authors of *Respectful Parents, Respectful Kids*; *The Compassionate Classroom*; and *The No-Fault Classroom*—all based on Nonviolent Communication and translated into numerous languages. In addition, Victoria and Sura have developed *The No-Fault Zone Game*—a communication and conflict resolution tool used in homes and classrooms throughout the world.

Sura Hart is an educator, author, and certified trainer with the international Center for Nonviolent Communication and worldwide leader in the incorporation of the proven process of Nonviolent Communication in school communities. She offers Compassionate Classroom and No-Fault Zone workshops and trainings throughout the world—in the United States, Canada, Europe, Central America, Australia, and China.

When not traveling, Sura makes her home in Seattle, Washington, where she enjoys spending time with her family and coaching educators and parents in collaborative communication skills and restorative conflict resolution. **www.TheNoFaultZone.com**

Victoria Kindle Hodson, teacher, consultant, and internationally recognized author, is a passionate proponent of respectful interactions between adults and young people. For four decades, she has been sharing compassionate practices from the fields of parenting, education, positive psychology, and brain science with thousands of parents, teachers, and students.

Victoria lives in Ventura, California, where she is currently training teachers in *The No-Fault Zone* curriculum, designing professional development programs for personalizing classroom instruction, and working with private clients. **www.TheNoFaultZone.com**